ESSEN PHYSICS FOR STANDARD GRADE

by

Arthur Gibbons

© *A. Gibbons, 1994.*
ISBN 0 7169 3191 5

The author is the Examination Officer responsible for Physics at the Scottish Examination Board. However, the views expressed in this book are his own and do not emanate from the Board.

ROBERT GIBSON · Publisher
17 Fitzroy Place, Glasgow, G3 7SF.

PREFACE

This book has been written for students who have decided to follow the Standard Grade Physics course.

The book provides a summary of all the basic knowledge which is needed for the General Level and Credit Level examinations in Standard Grade Physics.

The book also gives information on the types of question which are used in question papers to test knowledge and understanding of the content of the Standard Grade Physics course.

Worked examples of calculations are provided. Revision questions with answers and a summary list of all the relationships which are needed for Standard Grade Physics are also included.

CONTENTS

INTRODUCTION

Capital questions

What is the capital city of France?

This question tests your knowledge of capital cities.

Unless you actually know the name of the capital of France you will never be able to answer the question. You **cannot** work out the answer to this question. You **can** work out what the answer is **not**! For example, you may know that Edinburgh is the capital of Scotland and that Lisbon is the capital of Portugal. Therefore, you can deduce that the capital of France is neither of these two cities.

However, unless the actual name of the capital of France resides in your memory you will have to 'pass' on this question.
It is impossible to know the capital of France without knowing!

If you want to be a 'mastermind' and your specialist subject is capital cities of the world, then there is no easy way. You have to learn and commit to memory Paris, Rome, London, Edinburgh, Buenos Aires, Bangkok and a whole host of others.

Physics facts

So it is with Standard Grade Physics. If you want to do well in your chosen subject, then there are basic facts that you need to know. In addition, it is important that you have a good understanding of these facts. There is no easy route to acquiring this basic knowledge and understanding that is needed to master physics. There is no short cut. The basic rules of the subject, the essential facts, the fundamental principles all have to be learned.

Face up to a fact of physics. In order to do physics you need to collect together a basic tool kit. This tool kit includes the things which have to be remembered. It also includes the ability to do physics calculations. In addition, the tool kit includes being able to describe and explain situations where physics principles are at work. Recalling, calculating, describing and explaining are the basic tools that you need for doing Standard Grade Physics.

Knowledge needed

The Standard Grade Physics course consists of seven Units. The Units are concerned with Telecommunication, Using Electricity, Health Physics, Electronics, Transport, Energy Matters and Space Physics. There are facts to be learned, calculations to be done and explanations and descriptions to be given on the content of each of the Units.

For the Credit Level Physics examination, there are over 300 'capital cities' which have to be learned. Around 200 of these need to be known for the General Level examination. This book covers all of the 'capital cities' — everything you need to know for the examinations.

K&U Kit

If you look at a question paper for Standard Grade Physics you will notice that the marks for the questions are allocated to two columns.

One of the columns is headed K&U — this stands for knowledge and understanding. The other column is headed PS which stands for problem solving.

	K&U	PS

On a visit to the optician to have her eyes tested, Susan was told that each lens in her new spectacles would have a power of + 1·5 D.

(*a*) Calculate the focal length of each lens.

(*b*) Is Susan long sighted or short sighted?

(*c*) Describe an experi~~

one ~~ ~~

The questions whose marks are allocated to the K&U column are designed to test whether you are equipped with the basic tool kit for physics. The questions whose marks are assigned to the PS column test your ability to use this tool kit in solving physics problems.

Problem solving in physics is dependent on knowing the facts. You can never hope to solve problems in physics if you have no fundamental knowledge and understanding of physics.

A job cannot be done without the tools. This is why mastery of the facts is so important. You cannot answer questions on capital cities of countries unless you know the capital cities!

This book will help you to get to grips with what has to be known and understood for Standard Grade Physics. The book is designed to provide you with a do-it-yourself K&U kit!

Showing knowing

If you want to test a person's knowledge of capital cities, you ask questions on capital cities! Similarly, if you want to check up on a person's knowledge and understanding of physics at Standard Grade, you ask questions on Standard Grade Physics.

When you have the knowledge and understanding which is required for Standard Grade Physics, this means that you can recall certain facts. You can also do basic physics calculations and you can give descriptions and explanations of situations where physics principles are at work.

You show that you have knowledge and understanding of physics by the way in which you respond to the questions in the examination papers or in class tests. The questions will be asked in a way which will prompt you to show that you can recall, calculate, describe and explain.

Recall-questions

Questions which test your ability to recall basic facts will usually begin with the words 'State ...', 'Name ...', 'Give ...', 'Draw ...'.

These questions are prompting you to give a short, snappy fact of physics. For example, 'State the frequency of the mains supply.' or 'Draw the circuit symbol for a resistor.' are questions which are prompting you to write '50 hertz' and draw '—⟦⟧—'.

Calculating-questions

Questions which prompt you to do a basic calculation are easy to recognise. More often than not, they will begin with 'Calculate ...'.

If you have acquired the necessary knowledge, then it will be obvious to you exactly what has to be calculated. Data will be provided in these questions. Thereafter, you will recall a physics formula, correctly insert the data in the formula, do the arithmetic and provide the correct answer and units.

The following question is designed to test your ability to carry out a calculation.

> A sound of frequency 1320 hertz is transmitted through the air at a speed of 330 metres per second. Calculate the wavelength of the sound.

This question is prompting you to calculate a wavelength. First of all you have to recall the correct physics formula. The formula which should be

7

residing in your memory and which should spring from your mind and on to the page is this one

$$\text{speed of sound} = \text{frequency} \times \text{wavelength}$$

Thereafter, you insert the data into the formula and do some mathematics as follows

$$\begin{aligned} \text{wavelength} &= \frac{\text{speed of sound}}{\text{frequency}} \\ &= \frac{330}{1320} \\ &= \frac{1}{4} \\ &= 0 \cdot 25 \text{ metres} \end{aligned}$$

Describing-questions

Questions which test your ability to describe are also easy to identify. More often than not they begin with 'Describe ...'.

Giving descriptions involves painting a picture in words of what you see. Descriptions may also include diagrams. A diagram can be worth a thousand words! Descriptions do not include giving reasons or explanations for what you see. They involve you in writing down accurate statements of what you have observed.

For example, the following question should prompt you to give a picture in words, perhaps with the aid of a diagram, of how you would go about measuring the speed of sound.

Describe a method of measuring the speed of sound.

In giving your description, you draw on your knowledge and understanding of a way to making a measurement of the speed of sound. This description should be part of your basic K&U kit.

Your description would depend on what method you had committed to memory. You would perhaps write about watching for the smoke from a starting pistol and then listening for the bang.

You would go on to describe how the time between the sound and the bang would be measured, i.e. starting a stopwatch when you see the smoke and stopping it when you hear the bang. The distance between the pistol and the listener would also be measured.

The speed of sound would then be estimated using the relationship $\text{speed} = \dfrac{\text{distance}}{\text{time}}$. A number of measurements could be made so that an average time could be calculated.

Explaining-questions

Questions which test your ability to give explanations usually begin with 'Explain ...'.

Explanations go deeper than descriptions. Explanations look beneath the surface. They are concerned with more than just painting a picture in words of what you observe.

Explanations involve you in giving reasons for what you see. Explanations will involve you in accounting for what is going on in terms of physics principles. Explanations may also include diagrams.

The following question should prompt you to give an explanation.

Explain how the curved dish used in a TV aerial helps to increase the strength of the TV signal received from a satellite.

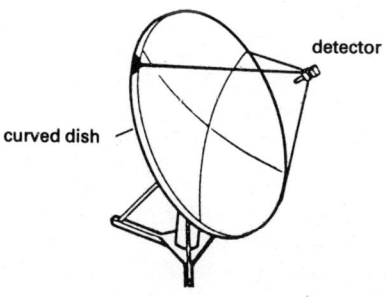

9

The explanation which is prompted by this question should be part of your K&U kit. This explanation should reside in your memory and you might respond along the following lines.

> The curved dish collects the TV waves which would otherwise pass by the detector of the aerial. The dish reflects these waves back towards the detector. The curved dish causes the waves to be brought to a focus at the detector. The collection and focusing of the waves thereby increases the strength of the signal in the detector.

In answering this question you are doing more than simply giving a description. You are accounting for what is happening in a dish aerial in terms of the principles of physics.

About this book

This book is more of a memo-pad than a text book.

It is not the intention of the book to provide lots of background material with illustrations and examples. Its purpose is to provide you with a K&U kit. It is a book which is designed to cover only the essential, fundamental knowledge and understanding which is required for the Standard Grade Physics examinations.

There is a chapter for each of the seven Units which make up the Standard Grade Physics syllabus. Each chapter is divided into sections. Within each section there is a list of content to be covered.

For each item in the list of content there are numbered paragraphs. The paragraphs give the detail of what has to be known and understood about the content for the General and Credit Level examinations. The paragraphs give the facts which you are expected to be able to state. They give examples of the kind of calculations you should be able to carry out. They also give the descriptions, the explanations and the diagrams which may be required of you in the examination.

The book also has a chapter which includes K&U questions. You can try the questions in this chapter to check up on the extent of your knowledge and understanding of the content of Standard Grade Physics

Using the book

☆ Use the book along with other text books and notes from your teacher to aid your understanding.

☆ Use the book as a revision aid. Use it as means of refreshing your memory of the fundamental facts.

☆ Use the book as a checklist which can be ticked off when a new piece of knowledge is gained and understood.

☆ Use the book to keep a check on the pace of your learning.

☆ Use the book to pin-point any areas where you are having difficulty. Discuss these with your teacher.

☆ Use the book to test your knowledge and understanding of the content of Standard Grade Physics.

Practice makes perfect

The Standard Grade Physics course runs over a period of two years. This means that you should be learning a new 'capital city' roughly every half hour. Some are easy and some are quite tricky. Do not leave them all to the last minute. Face up to the facts now!

Practice makes perfect. Close the book. Are you in possession of the knowledge which is needed? Test yourself by trying practice questions and questions from Standard Grade Physics question papers.

What is the capital city of France?

UNIT 1 — TELECOMMUNICATION

The table below lists the sections and content of the Unit on Telecommuncation.

Section	Content
1. Communication through the air and through wires	Speed of sound
	Communicating with wires between transmitter and receiver
	Telephone and audio signals
2. Waves	Frequency, wavelength, amplitude and speed
3. Radio and television	Radio and television waves
	Radio receiver
	Radio transmission
	Radio waves, wavelength and frequency bands
	Television receiver
	TV transmission and reception
	Black and white TV picture
	Colour picture
4. Optical fibres	Optical fibre transmissions
	Communication by copper cable and glass fibre
	Laws of reflection
5. Satellites and dish aerials	Satellites
	Dish aerials

The paragraphs in italics describe the additional knowledge which is needed for the Credit Level examination.

SECTION 1:

COMMUNICATION THROUGH THE AIR AND THROUGH WIRES

Speed of sound

1. The speed of sound is very much less than the speed of light. Evidence of this is provided by thunder and lightning. The thunder and lightning are produced more or less at the same time. However, you hear the sound of thunder some seconds after you see the light from the lightning flash.

2. You are expected to be able to describe a method of measuring the speed of sound. One way of doing this is already described in the Introduction in the section entitled 'Describing-questions'. Another method of making the measurement is described below. The method involves the use of microphones and electronic timing equipment.

Two microphones are placed a measured distance apart. The microphones are connected through an electronic switch to a timer as shown in the diagram below.

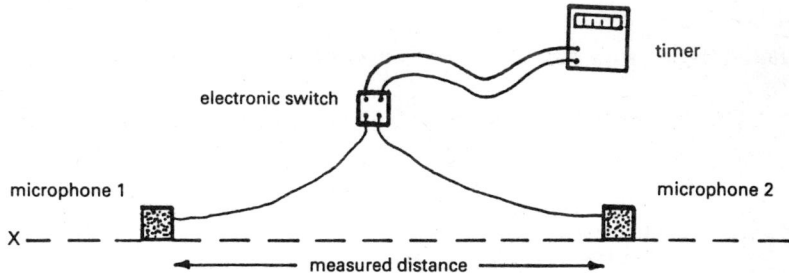

Two wooden blocks are banged together at position X so that a sound is produced. When the sound reaches microphone 1 the timer starts timing. When the sound reaches microphone 2 the timer is stopped. The reading on the timer is the time taken for the sound to travel the measured distance. The values of the measured distance and the reading on the timer are inserted into the relationship speed $= \dfrac{\text{distance}}{\text{time}}$ and the speed of sound is calculated. The experiment is repeated so that a number of measurements are made and an average value calculated.

3. Do calculations on sound transmission using the following relationship.

$$\text{speed} = \frac{\text{distance}}{\text{time}}$$

$$v = \frac{d}{t}$$

The distance 'd' is measured in metres, the time 't' in seconds and the speed in metres per second.

An example of the kind of calculating that might be expected of you is as follows.

> How far away is the lightning if the thunder is heard 5 seconds after the flash is seen? The speed of sound is 330 metres per second.

$$v = \frac{d}{t}$$

$d = v \times t$
$\quad = 330 \times 5$
$\quad = 1650 \text{ metres}$

distance from lightning = 1650 metres

Communicating with wires between transmitter and receiver

4. A circuit consisting of a battery, bulb and switch is one way of sending a coded message over a distance.

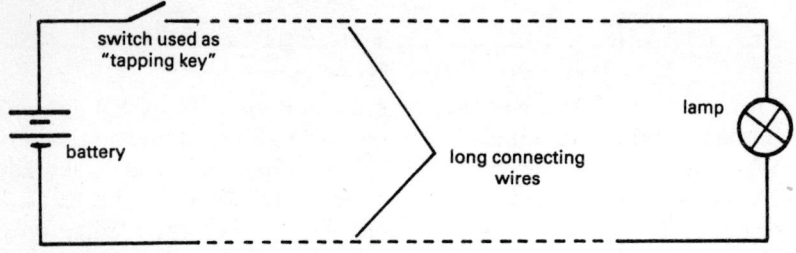

Close and open the switch. Short flashes from the bulb could be the dots of the Morse code and long flashes could signal the dashes.

14

The switch end is the transmitting part of the system and the bulb is the receiving end.

Two advantages of sending messages by wires, rather than by sound, are privacy and quickness of transmission.

Telephone and audio signals

5. A telephone is an example of long range communication using wires. The mouthpiece of the telephone has a microphone. The earpiece contains an earphone which acts like small loudspeaker.

6. Sound waves are changed to electrical audio signals by a microphone. Audio signals are changed to sound waves by a loudspeaker.

7. In a telephone, electrical audio signals are transmitted from the mouthpiece along communicating wires.

   The audio signals in the communicating wires of a telephone travel at a speed close to 300 000 000 metres per second. This speed is very much greater than the speed of sound — almost a million times greater.

8. *The loudness of the sound at the microphone affects the strength of the audio signal in the communicating wire. Loud sounds produce strong electrical audio signals. The audio signals in the wire are affected by the frequency of the sound at the microphone. High frequency sounds at the microphone produce high frequency audio signals in the communicating wires.*

9. The audio signals of loud and soft sounds are displayed on an oscilloscope screen as shown in the diagram below.

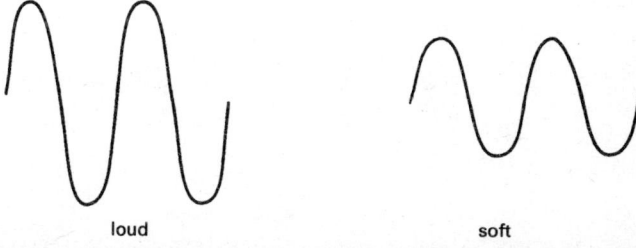

loud   soft

The louder the sound the greater the amplitude of the audio signal.

15

Low and high frequency audio signals are displayed on an oscilloscope screen as shown in the diagram below.

low
frequency

high
frequency

The higher the frequency of the sound the closer the spacing of the audio signal pattern.

10. If the frequency of one sound is double that of another, the sounds are said to be an octave apart. For example, in a musical scale — doh, ray, me, fah, soh, lah, te, doh — high doh has double the frequency of low doh. The high doh and the low doh are one octave apart.

SECTION 2: WAVES

Frequency, wavelength, amplitude and speed

1. Signals can be transmitted by means of waves. Waves transmit energy.

2. Waves are described in terms of frequency, wavelength and amplitude.

Frequency (f) is the number of waves produced per second — frequency is measured in hertz (Hz).

Wavelength (λ) is the length of one wave. Wavelength is measured in metres (m).

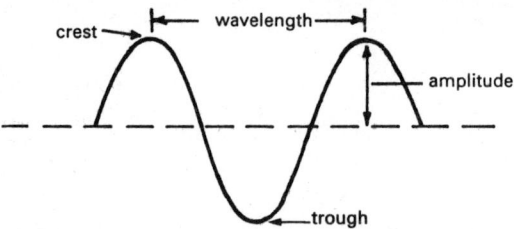

crest

wavelength

amplitude

trough

Amplitude is the height of a wave, i.e. half the vertical distance between a crest and a trough. Amplitude is measured in metres.

16

3. Do calculations involving distance, time and speed for water waves. You need to remember the relationship, speed $= \dfrac{\text{distance}}{\text{time}}$, i.e. $v = \dfrac{d}{t}$, in order to do these calculations.

An example of the kind of calculating that might be expected of you is as follows.

> The crest of a water wave in a pond travels a distance of 1·8 metres in 6 seconds. What is the speed of the water wave?

$v = \dfrac{d}{t}$

$ = \dfrac{1 \cdot 8}{6}$

$ = 0 \cdot 3$ metres per second

speed of water wave $= 0 \cdot 3$ metres per second

4. You are expected to do calculations involving speed, wavelength and frequency for water and sound waves. You need to remember the following relationship in order to do these calculations.

$$\text{wave speed} = \text{frequency} \times \text{wavelength}$$
$$v = f\lambda$$

Speed is measured in metres per second, frequency is measured in hertz and wavelength is measured in metres.

An example of the kind of calculating that might be expected of you is as follows.

> A whistle produces a sound of frequency 1000 hertz. The speed of sound is 330 metres per second. Calculate the wavelength of this sound.

$v = f\lambda$

$\lambda = \dfrac{v}{f}$

$ = \dfrac{330}{1000}$

$ = 0 \cdot 33$ metres

wavelength of sound $= 0 \cdot 33$ metres

5. *At Credit Level, you are expected to be able to prove that wave speed equals frequency × wavelength, i.e. v = fλ. You could do this as follows.*

   Suppose a wave has a frequency f. This means that f waves are produced every second. Therefore, the time taken to produce one wave is $\frac{1}{f}$ seconds. The wave travels a distance of one wavelength (λ) in this time.

$$speed\ (v) = \frac{distance\ travelled\ by\ wave}{time\ taken}$$

$$= \frac{1\ wavelength}{time\ to\ travel\ 1\ wavelength}$$

$$= \frac{\lambda}{\frac{1}{f}}$$

$$= f\lambda$$

SECTION 3:   RADIO AND TELEVISION

Radio and television waves

1. Radio and television transmissions are examples of long range communication which do not use wires to connect the transmitter to the receiver.

2. Radio and television transmissions can be thought of as waves. The radio and television waves transmit energy.

3. Radio and television waves travel at very high speed. Their speed is 300 000 000 metres per second.

4. *At Credit Level you are expected to do calculations involving distance, time and speed for radio and television waves. This is the same type of calculation as you did for water waves in Section 2: Waves, paragraph 3, except that the numbers will be a bit more awkward.*

18

An example of the kind of calculating that might be expected of you is as follows.

> *How long will it take a radio wave to travel directly from Aberdeen to Dundee, a distance of 87 km?*

speed of radio wave equals 300 000 000 m/s

$$v = \frac{d}{t}$$

$$t = \frac{d}{v}$$

$$= \frac{87\,000}{300\,000\,000}$$

$$= 0{\cdot}00029\,s$$

time taken = 290 microseconds

Radio receiver

5. The main parts of a radio receiver are the aerial, tuner, decoder, amplifier, loudspeaker and electricity supply.

   Make sure that you can identify each of these main parts on a block diagram of a radio receiver such as the one shown below.

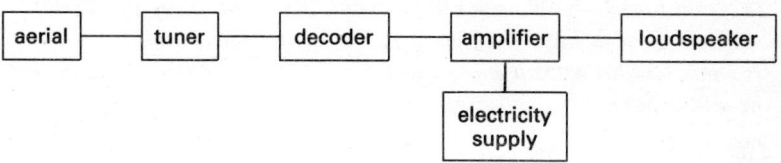

6. The aerial of the radio receiver detects radio waves and converts these into high frequency electrical signals.

   The tuner selects the electrical signals which come from the radio station whose broadcast a listener wants to hear.

   The decoder filters out the audio part of the high frequency electrical signal and passes this to the amplifier.

   The amplifier boosts the audio signal and passes the boosted signal to the loudspeaker.

   The electricity supply provides the energy for the amplified audio signals.

   The loudspeaker converts the electrical audio signals into sound waves.

Radio transmission

7. *A way of transmitting audio signals by radio waves is described as follows.*

   In a radio transmitter, a high frequency electrical signal is produced. Audio signals from a microphone connected to the transmitter are combined with the high frequency signal. The audio signal from the microphone changes the amplitude of the high frequency electrical signal. A combined signal is produced as shown by the diagrams below.

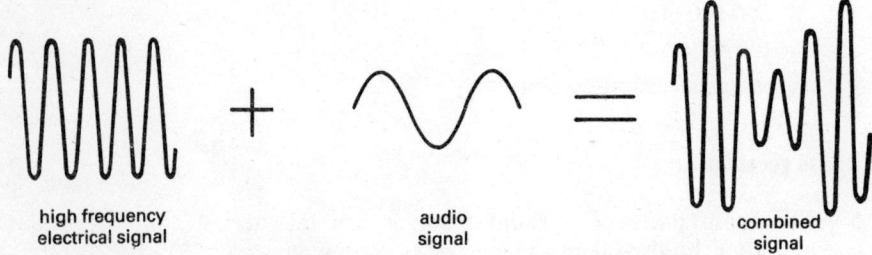

high frequency   audio   combined
electrical signal   signal   signal

   This method of combining an audio signal with the high frequency radio signal is called amplitude modulation.

   The combined signal is amplified and sent out from the aerial of the transmitter as a high frequency radio wave. The amplitude of the high frequency radio wave is modulated in such a way that it acts as a carrier of the audio signal.

   The amplitude modulated wave is picked up by the aerial of a receiver which is tuned to the frequency of the carrier radio wave.

Radio waves, wavelengths and frequency bands.

8. A radio transmitter can be identified by either its broadcast wavelength or frequency, e.g. Radio 1, 99·5 megahertz; Radio Scotland, 370 metres.

9. *Do calculations involving speed, frequency and wavelength of radio waves. To do these calculations, you have to remember that the relationship, speed = frequency × wavelength, i.e. $v = f\lambda$, can be applied to radio waves. You also need to remember the value for the speed of radio waves.*

An example of the kind of calculating that might be expected of you is as follows.

Radio Scotland transmits on a frequency of 810 kHz. Calculate the wavelength of the transmitted wave.

$v = f\lambda$

$\lambda = \dfrac{v}{f}$

$= \dfrac{300\ 000\ 000}{810\ 000}$

$= 370\ metres$

wavelength of transmitted wave = 370 metres

10. *Waves with a long wavelength diffract more than waves with a short wavelength. This means that they bend round obstacles to a greater extent than short wavelength waves. The diffraction of long wavelength and short wavelength waves round an obstacle is shown in the diagrams below.*

long wavelength   short wavelength

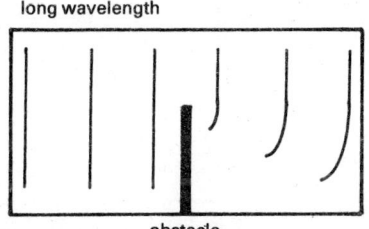 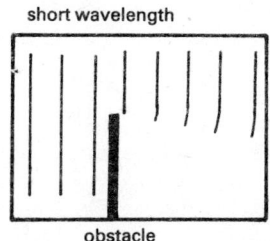

obstacle   obstacle

Radio waves generally have longer wavelength than TV waves. Radio waves, therefore, bend round obstacles, such as hills, to a greater extent and tend to be able to reach places that TV waves cannot. Hence radio transmissions can often give good reception in areas where TV reception is poor.

11. *Radio waves are grouped into bands according to their wavelengths or frequencies. The waves in the different bands have different properties. This makes the waves suited to different uses.*

For example, the long waveband and medium waveband have wavelengths which can diffract round obstacles. This means that the waves are suited to good reception in hilly areas. In addition, the waves can be reflected from a charged layer in the upper atmosphere. This means that they can be used for transmitting over long distances.

21

The wavelengths of the short waveband do not diffract to the same extent as the waves in the medium and long wavebands. The short-wavelength waves, therefore, require line of sight transmission. This limits their range. Such waves, however, are especially suited to high quality, stereo-sound transmissions.

Television receiver

12. The main parts of a TV receiver are the aerial, tuner, audio decoder, video decoder, audio amplifier, video amplifier, TV tube, loudspeaker and electricity supply.

    Make sure that you can identify each of these parts on a block diagram of a TV receiver such as the one shown below.

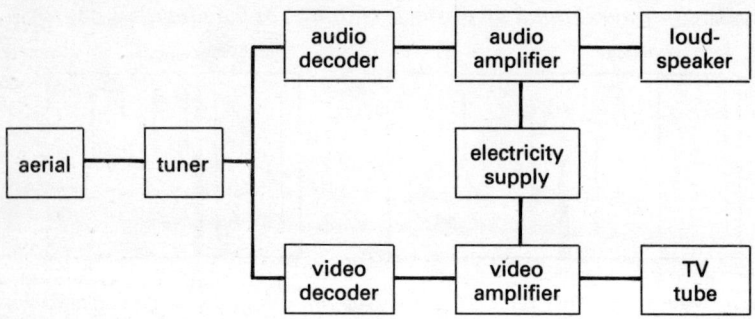

13. The aerial of the TV receiver detects TV waves and converts these into high frequency electrical signals.

    The tuner selects the electrical signals of the transmission which the viewer wants to see.

    The audio decoder filters out the audio part of the high frequency electrical signal and passes this to the audio amplifier.

    The video decoder filters out the video part of the high frquency electrical signal and passes this to the video amplifier.

The audio amplifier increases the strength of the audio part of the signal and passes it to the loudspeaker.

The video amplifier increases the strength of the video part of the signal and passes it to the TV tube.

The electricity supply provides the energy for the amplified audio and video signals.

The loudspeaker converts the audio signals into sound waves.

The TV tube converts the video signals into a picture on a screen.

TV transmission and reception

14. *TV transmission and reception can be described as follows.*

In a TV transmitter, an ultra high frequency electrical signal is combined with a video signal and an audio signal. The combined signal is amplified and sent out from the aerial of the TV transmitter as a TV wave. The TV wave is modulated in such a way that it acts as a carrier for both video signal and audio signal.

The modulated wave is picked up by the aerial of the TV receiver, which is tuned to the frequency of the carrier TV wave. The video signal and the audio signal are separated from the modulated carrier wave. This is called demodulation. The video and audio signals are then amplified. The amplified video signal produces a picture on the screen of the TV tube. The amplified audio signal is converted to sound waves by the receiver's loudspeaker.

Black and white TV picture

15. A picture on a black and white TV is produced by an electron beam in the TV tube striking a phosphor-coated screen. When the beam strikes the screen, it causes the phosphor on the screen to emit light. The beam moves backwards and forwards and up and down the screen as shown in the diagram on the following page. This is called scanning.

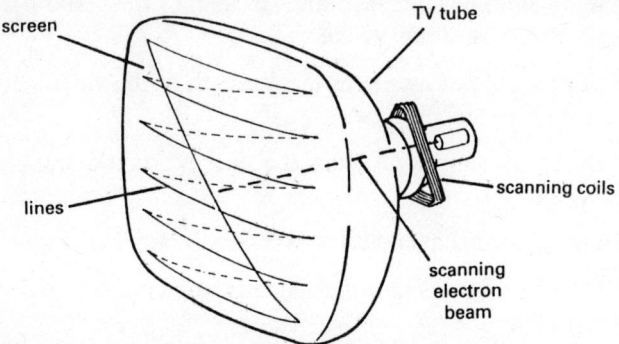

The video signal varies the number of electrons in the beam striking the screen. This, in turn, varies the brightness of the light coming from the phosphor on the screen. Various shades from black to grey to white can therefore be displayed on the screen.

The scanning beam produces a picture which is made up of lines. A line on the screen is made up of bits which vary in brightness from black to grey to white. Each line on the screen is a slice of the TV picture. When all of the lines are built up together a complete picture can be seen on the screen.

16. *A picture which shows movement on a TV screen is just a series of still pictures which are being shown rapidly, one after the other. Each still picture is built up from lines which are traced onto a phosphor-coated screen by an electron beam.*

The video signal varies the strength of the electron beam which, in turn, varies the brightness of the light coming from the phosphor on the screen. A line on the screen is therefore made up of bits which vary in brightness from black to grey to white.

The phosphor on the screen continues to glow after each line is traced. This glow lasts long enough for the eye to recognise the complete picture which is built up from all of the lines which are traced on to the screen by the beam.

The still picture is replaced by another which shows the next bit of the movement. This picture is replaced by another and so on. The eye interprets what is being shown on this rapid sequence of still pictures as a smooth movement.

24

Colour picture

17. All the colours which can be seen on the screen of a colour TV can be obtained by mixing red, green and blue light.

    Red, green and blue light can be mixed to produce white light. Other mixes of red, green and blue light can produce the following colours.

    > *blue + green = turquoise*
    > *blue + red   = magenta*
    > *green + red = yellow*

SECTION 4:   OPTICAL FIBRES

Optical fibre transmissions

1. An optical fibre is a very thin, flexible rod of pure glass through which light can be transmitted very quickly.

   Optical fibres can be used in telecommunication systems. For example, the electrical audio signals from a telephone can be changed into light signals which can then be transmitted along a length of optical fibre. The light signals are transmitted along the fibre at very high speed. The light in the optical fibre can be detected at the receiving end of the system by a photodiode. The photodiode changes the light signals back into electrical, audio signals. The audio signals are then changed into sound waves.

Communication by copper cable and glass fibre

2. Copper cable as well as optical fibre is used in communication systems, e.g. telephone communication.

   Communication using optical fibre offers advantages over communication using copper cable.

   One advantage is cost. The copper in a cable is expensive whereas the glass of an optical fibre is plentiful and cheaper. The weight of a kilometre of optical fibre is very much less than the weight of a kilometre of copper cable and this makes the optical fibre easier to lay.

25

Another advantage of optical fibre communication is that the light signal in the glass is not affected by electrical interference.

In addition, there is very little loss of signal strength in transmissions using optical fibres. The signal reaching the receiver in an optical fibre system therefore tends to be of better quality.

3. *Do calculations on signal transmission using light. In carrying out such calculations, you will have to remember that speed of the signal transmission $= \dfrac{distance\ travelled}{time\ taken}$, i.e. $v = \dfrac{d}{t}$.*

An example of the type of calculating that might be expected of you is as follows.

> *The speed of a light signal in an optical fibre cable is 200 000 km/s. Calculate the time taken for the signal to travel a distance of 50 km in the cable.*

$$v = \frac{d}{t}$$

$$t = \frac{d}{v}$$

$$= \frac{50}{200\ 000}$$

$$= 0.00025\ s$$

time taken for light signal $= 0.00025\ s$

Laws of reflection

4. Light can be reflected. An example of this is light bouncing off the surface of a plane mirror. The light is reflected from the mirror surface according to certain rules or laws.

    One of the rules for reflection is that the angle at which a ray of light strikes the mirror will equal the angle at which it is reflected. This is shown in the diagram.

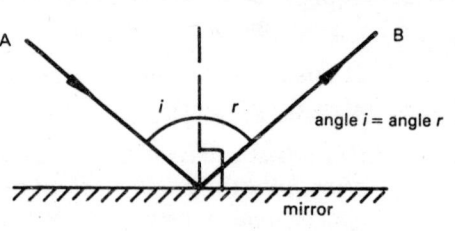

Another rule is that the path followed by light is reversible. This means that if a ray is redirected along the path followed by ray B it will follow the path of ray A.

5. *The rules governing the reflection of light apply to the transmission of light in an optical fibre system. The light in the optical fibre is reflected internally as shown in the diagram below.*

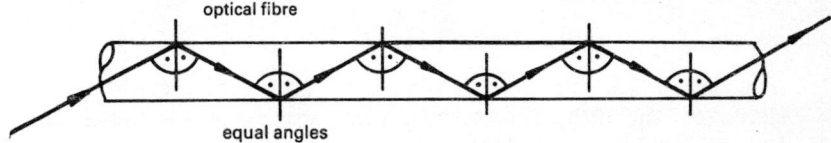

Repeated internal reflections enable the light to bounce its way along inside the optical fibre.

SECTION 5:   SATELLITES AND DISH AERIALS

Satellites

1. The time taken for a satellite to make one complete revolution of the earth is called the period of the satellite. The period of a satellite is dependent on the height of the satellite's orbit.

2. A geostationary satellite has an orbit such that the satellite is always above the same point on the earth's surface. The period of a geostationary satellite's orbit is 24 hours — the time taken for the earth to make one complete rotation.

3. Ground stations on different continents on the earth can communicate with each other via geostationary satellites as shown in this diagram.

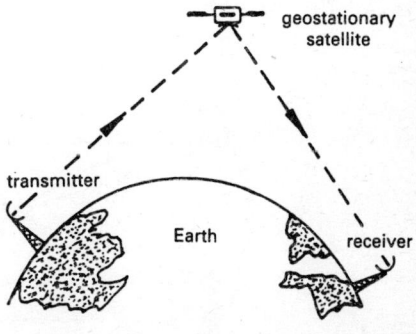

A radio wave is transmitted from a ground station and is received by the geostationary satellite. The satellite retransmits the wave back down to earth where it can be picked up by the receiving station. The satellite provides a link which allows communication between stations which are hidden from each other by the curvature of the earth.

Dish aerials

4. The curved reflector of a dish aerial increases the strength of the signal in the aerial's detector.

An explanation for this is as follows.

The curved dish collects the TV waves which would otherwise pass by the detector. The dish reflects these waves back towards the detector as shown in the diagram below.

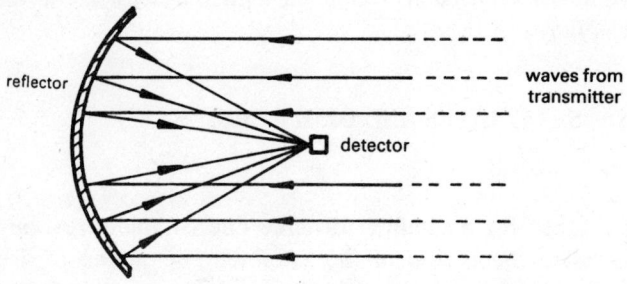

The curved dish causes the waves to be brought to a focus at the detector. The collection and focusing of the waves by the dish thereby increases the strength of the signal in the detector.

5. *Curved reflectors are also used in transmitters of radio and TV waves.*

In the transmitter the source of the waves is placed at the focus of the curved reflector as shown in the diagram below.

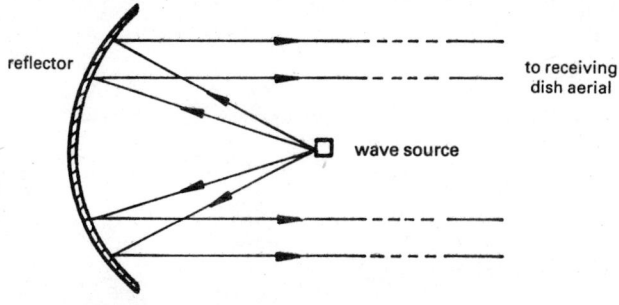

28

The transmitted wave is formed into a narrow beam as a result of its reflection from the curved dish. This means that most of the energy of the source can be transmitted to the receiving aerial.

6. An example of the use of curved reflectors in telecommunication is as follows.

    Curved reflectors are used for sending and receiving telephone calls. This is done by line of sight radio links between aerials placed on high towers.

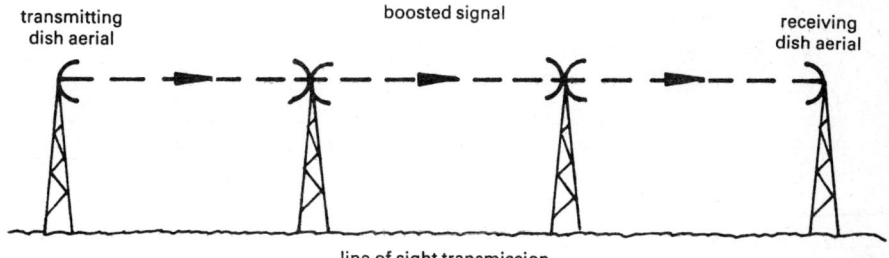

line of sight transmission

The curved dish on the transmitter tower sends out a narrow beam of radio waves to a receiving tower some 40 km distant. The radio waves act as a carrier for the telephone call.

At the receiving tower, another curved dish is used to collect the radio signal. The signal is then boosted for onward transmission to the next receiving station. This process is repeated until the call reaches its final destination.

UNIT 2 — USING ELECTRICITY

The table below lists the sections and content of the Unit on Using Electricity.

Section	Content
1. From the wall socket	Household appliances
	Flex and fuse
	Safety and earth wire
2. Alternating and direct current	Mains and battery
	Circuit symbols
	Charge, current and voltage
3. Electrical resistance and power	Ammeter and voltmeter
	Resistance
	Variable resistor
	Power
	Lamps and heaters
4. Useful circuits	Series and parallel circuits
	Fault finding circuit
5. Behind the wall	Mains supply
	Ring circuit
	Lighting circuit
	Fuses and circuit breakers
	Metering energy
6. Movement from electricity	Magnetic effect
	Electric motor

The paragraphs in italics describe the additional knowledge which is needed for the Credit Level examination.

SECTION 1:   FROM THE WALL SOCKET

Household appliances

1. Batteries and the mains supply are sources of energy.

    Electrical household appliances are connected to the mains supply. Electrical appliances transfer energy from the mains supply and produce heat, light, sound or movement.

    For example, a three-bar electric fire transfers energy from the mains supply. It is an appliance which is designed to produce heat. The electric fire also provides some light but its main purpose is to produce heat.

    An electric lamp also transfers energy from the mains supply. The purpose of an electric lamp is to produce light. However, it also produces heat.

    A food mixer transfers energy from the mains supply. It is an example of an electrical appliance which is designed to produce movement.

2. Different electrical appliances have different power ratings. This means that in one second they transfer different amounts of energy from the mains supply. Power is measured in watts.

    Typical power ratings of some electrical appliances are as follows.

Electric blanket	150 watts
Kettle	2 000 watts
TV	120 watts
Toaster	900 watts
Lamp	100 watts

Flex and fuse

3. The thickness of the flex for an appliance and the value of the fuse in its plug have to be selected so that both are suited to the power of the appliance.

31

You are expected to be able to select the appropriate flex and fuse for an electrical appliance. An example is as follows.

An electric iron has a power of 400 watts. What value of fuse and thickness of flex should be selected for the appliance?

Use the following information on power, flex thickness and fuse value given in the table below to help you make the selection.

Power rating of appliance in watts	Thickness of flex in square millimetres	Value of the fuse in amperes
Up to 720	0·5	3
720 to 1440	0·75	13
1440 to 2400	1·0	13
2400 to 3240	1·25	13

The power of the iron is in the 0 to 720 watts range. Therefore, a 0·5 mm^2 cable and a 3 A fuse should be selected.

4. The fuse in a plug is designed to protect the flex against the possibility of an electrical fault which could cause the flex to carry too much current.

5. The wires in a flex are coloured so that they can be identified. The wires and their colours are as follows.

live wire (brown); neutral wire (blue); earth wire (green and yellow)

6. Make sure that you are able to say to which pin the wires in a flex are connected in a plug, lampholder and extension socket. The diagrams below show the wires connected correctly.

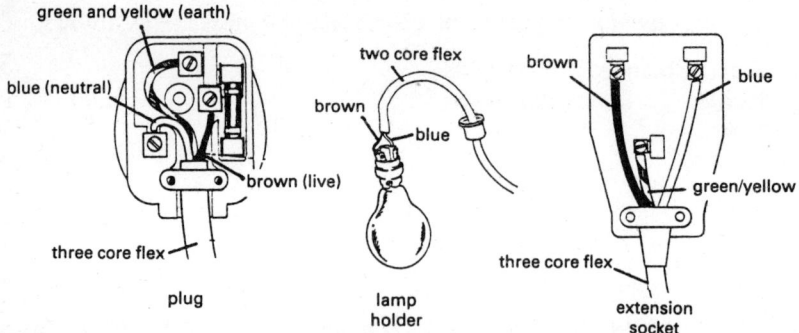

Unless the lampholder is made of metal, there is normally no need for an earth wire.

Safety and earth wire

7. The human body can conduct electricity. Moisture on the skin makes the body a better conductor than when the skin is dry. Care must be taken when using electricity.

Electricity is beneficial but if it is not treated with respect it can be dangerous. You are expected to be able to explain why situations involving electricity could lead to accidents. Some situations are given below.

An electric kettle should never be filled whilst it is plugged into the mains socket. Water is a conductor of electricity. Water on the adaptor of the kettle could provide an alternative path for the current and perhaps short circuit the mains supply. Worse still, wet hands near a live supply could provide a path for a current in a person's body which could prove fatal.

Badly worn flex is a hazard. If bare wire is exposed, there is a risk of a person's body making contact with a live wire and the person being electrocuted.

An accident could also occur if a fuse of too high a value is fitted to the plug of an appliance. This could permit a large current in the flex and cause overheating which could lead to a fire.

In addition, careless use of multi-way adaptors can draw too much current from the supply and produce overheating in the cable from the mains supply. The overheating could lead to a fire.

8. An earth wire is included in an electrical appliance as a safety device.

    The earth wire is connected to the casing of the appliance. The way in which the earth wire acts as a safety device can be explained as follows.

    Suppose for some reason a fault develops in the appliance such that the casing of the appliance makes contact with the live wire. If no earth wire is included and the casing is touched, this has the same effect as touching directly the live wire from the mains.

    The presence of the earth wire, however, prevents the casing from becoming live. The earth wire provides a low resistance path for the current from the live wire to earth. The current in the earth wire is large enough to blow the fuse in the plug of the appliance. The faulty appliance

33

is therefore disconnected from the mains supply. The appliance is no longer live and there is no danger of being electrocuted.

9. *Switches and fuses in electrical appliances are connected to the live wire. This is another safety precaution.*

This ensures that the appliance is disconnected from the mains when the appliance is switched off, or if its fuse has blown. When an appliance is disconnected from the live side of the mains supply, no part of the appliance can be live. This means that there is no danger of electrocution if a person touches any part of the appliance.

However, this would not be the case if the switch, for example, were connected to the neutral wire. In this situation an open switch 'switches off' the appliance but it does not disconnect the appliance from the live side of the supply.

This means that even although the appliance is 'switched off' there is still a possibility of an electric shock from the appliance. Switches and fuses connected in the live side of the supply guard against this possibility.

When there is no direct connection from the appliance to the live side of the mains supply, the appliance really is 'switched off'.

10. Some electrical appliances are designed so that they do not require an earth wire. These appliances are protected by a double layer of insulation. They carry a double insulation symbol, as shown below, to identify them.

Make sure you can recognise and draw the double insulation symbol.

SECTION 2:   ALTERNATING AND DIRECT CURRENT

Mains and battery

1. The mains supplies alternating current (a.c.). A battery supplies direct current (d.c.).

    Alternating current is current whose direction continuously changes in a regular way. First of all the current is in one direction. Then it is in the opposite direction and so on. The current alternates — it is therefore referred to as alternating current.

    Direct current, on the other hand, is always in the one direction. It does not alternate. The current is direct — it is therefore referred to as direct current.

2. The voltage of the mains alternates with a frequency of 50 hertz. The voltage of the mains is quoted as 240 volts.

3. *The value which is quoted for an alternating voltage is less than the peak value of the alternating voltage.*

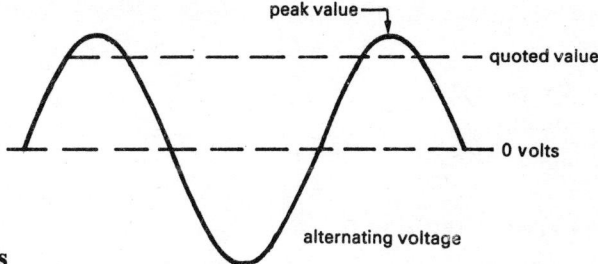

Circuit symbols

4. You are expected to be able to recognise and draw the circuit symbols shown below for a battery, fuse, lamp, switch, resistor, capacitor, diode, variable resistor.

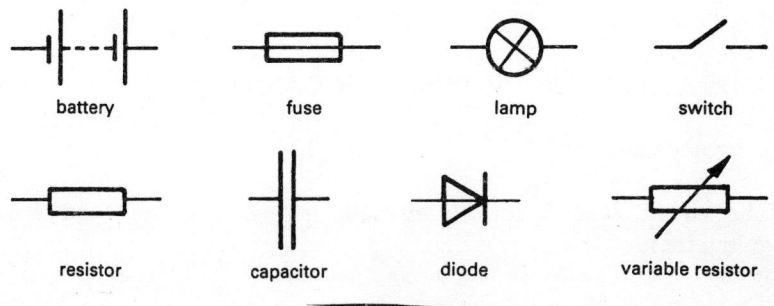

35

Charge, current and voltage

5. The outer electrons of the atoms of a conductor are free to move. The electrons are charged particles.

    Charge is measured in coulombs.

    When electrons move so that there is a flow of charge round a circuit, this is called an electric current. Electric current is measured in amperes.

6. *Carry out calculations involving the relationship between charge, current and time. The relationship which links these quantities is as follows.*

    $$charge = current \times time$$
    $$Q = It$$

    An example of the kind of calculating that might be expected of you is as follows.

    A conductor carries a current of 0·5 A. How much charge is moved through the conductor in a time of 10 s?

    $Q = It$
    $\quad = 0·5 \times 10$
    $\quad = 5\ coulombs$
    charge moved = 5 C

7. Voltage is measured in volts.

    When charges move round a circuit, the charges transfer energy from the electrical supply. The energy transferred by a coulomb of charge as it moves round a circuit is a measure of the voltage that is supplied to the circuit.

SECTION 3:   ELECTRICAL RESISTANCE AND POWER

Ammeter and voltmeter

1. The circuit symbol for an ammeter is —Ⓐ—. The symbol for a voltmeter is —Ⓥ—.

36

2. Make sure that you can draw circuit diagrams which show ammeters and voltmeters correctly positioned.

An ammeter is placed in **series** with that part of the circuit where the current is to be measured. A voltmeter is connected in **parallel** across that part of the circuit where the voltage is to be measured.

An example of a circuit which you might be expected to draw is as follows.

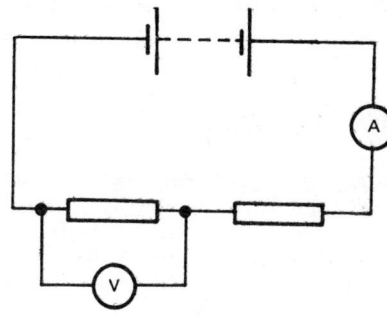

The ammeter is correctly positioned to measure the current from the battery. The voltmeter is correctly positioned to measure the voltage across one of the resistors in the circuit.

Resistance

3. The current which is drawn from the electrical supply in a circuit depends on the resistance of the circuit. If the resistance of a circuit is increased then the current in that circuit is decreased.

Resistance is measured in ohms.

4. Carry out calculations involving resistance, current and voltage. In carrying out these calculations, you will have to remember the relationship which links these quantities. The relationship is as follows.

$$\text{resistance} = \frac{\text{voltage}}{\text{current}}$$

$$R = \frac{V}{I}$$

An example of the kind of calculating that might be expected of you is as follows.

A battery of voltage 6 volts is connected across a length of wire which has a resistance of 12 ohms. Calculate the current in the wire.

$$R = \frac{V}{I}$$

$$I = \frac{V}{R}$$

$$= \frac{6}{12}$$

$$= 0{\cdot}5 \text{ ampere}$$

current in the wire $= 0{\cdot}5$ ampere

5. *For a given resistor, provided its temperature is kept fixed, the voltage, V, across the resistor divided by the current, I, in it is a constant.*

    This means that a doubling of the current in a resistor is accompanied by a doubling of the voltage across it. Three times the current is accompanied by three times the voltage and so on.

Variable resistor

6. A variable resistor is a resistor whose resistance can be varied. It can be used to control the size of the current in a circuit.

    You are expected to be able to give two examples of practical uses for variable resistors.

    One example of a practical use is in the volume control of a radio. Another use is in joysticks for computer games.

Power

7. Power is the rate of transferring energy. Power is defined by the following relationship.

$$\text{power} = \frac{\text{energy transferred}}{\text{time}}$$

$$P = \frac{E}{t}$$

Power is therefore measured in joules per second.

The watt is the unit of power. A power of 1 watt means that 1 joule of energy is being transferred every second.

The relationship for power can be rearranged as follows to give an expression for energy transferred in a time, t.

$$\text{energy transferred} = \text{power} \times \text{time}$$
$$E = Pt$$

8. When there is a current in a circuit, energy is being transferred.

You should be able to give three examples of circuits in the home where energy is being transferred by means of an electric current.

An electric iron is one example of such a circuit. The circuit for the iron consists mainly of a length of wire connected across the mains supply. When there is a current in the wire, energy is transferred and heat is produced.

An electric fire and a toaster are two other examples of circuits where the working component is a wire carrying a current. Energy is transferred and heat is produced by these two circuits.

9. The energy transferred every second by a circuit can be calculated by multiplying the voltage across the circuit and current in it.

$$\text{energy transferred per second} = VI$$
$$\text{power} = VI$$
$$P = VI$$

10. Carry out calculations involving the relationship between power, voltage and current.

An example of the kind of calculating that might be expected of you is as follows.

An electric toaster has a power of 960 watts. What is the current in the toaster when it is connected to a 240 volt supply?

$$P = VI$$
$$I = \frac{P}{V}$$
$$= \frac{960}{240}$$
$$= 4 \text{ amperes}$$

current in toaster = 4 amperes

11. *An alternative expression for power is I^2R. At Credit Level, you are expected to be able to prove that power = I^2R. You could do this as follows.*

Suppose a conductor of resistance R carries a current I and the voltage across the conductor is V.

$$R = \frac{V}{I}$$
$$V = IR$$
$$power = VI$$
$$= (IR)I$$
$$= I^2R$$

12. *Carry out calculations involving the following relationship.*

$$power = (current)^2 \times resistance$$
$$P = I^2R$$

An example of the kind of calculating that is expected of you is as follows.

A car vacuum cleaner has a resistance of 6 Ω. When connected to the car battery it draws a current of 2 A. Calculate the power of the cleaner.

$P = I^2R$
$\quad = 2 \times 2 \times 6$
$\quad = 24\,W$

Power of vacuum cleaner = 24 W

Lamps and heaters

13. In an electric lamp, energy is transferred as heat and light. An electric lamp can be of the filament or gas discharge type.

In the filament lamp, it is current in the filament which gives rise to the production of light. The gas discharge lamp has no filament. The gas in the lamp acts as a conductor. The current in the gas enables light and heat to be produced.

Gas discharge lamps are more efficient than filament lamps. They produce more visible light than filament lamps of the same power.

14. Electric heaters produce heat when there is current in the element of the heater. The element of the heater is a length of resistance wire.

SECTION 4: USEFUL CIRCUITS

Series and parallel circuits

1. In a series circuit the current is the same at all points in the circuit.

2. In a parallel circuit the current from the supply is the sum of the currents in the parallel branches.

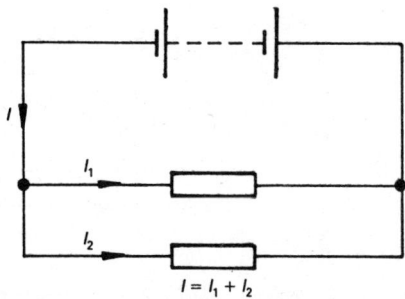

A number of electrical appliances connected by means of an adaptor to a mains socket, is an example of a circuit with parallel branches. The current drawn from the mains socket is the sum of the currents in each of the appliances. This arrangement may cause a large current to be drawn from the socket and could lead to overheating of the mains cables.

3. In a series circuit, the sum of the voltages across each of the components in the circuit is equal to the voltage of the supply.

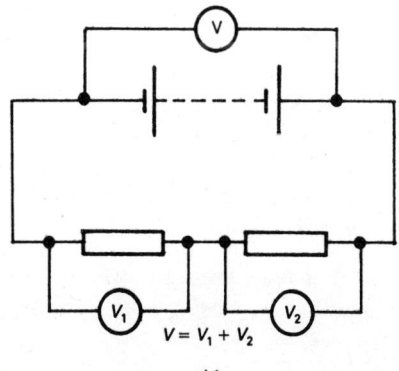

41

4. Where components are connected in parallel with each other, the voltage across each component is the same.

5. There are many appliances in the home which use two or more switches to connect components in series and in parralled. A two-bar electric fire is an example.

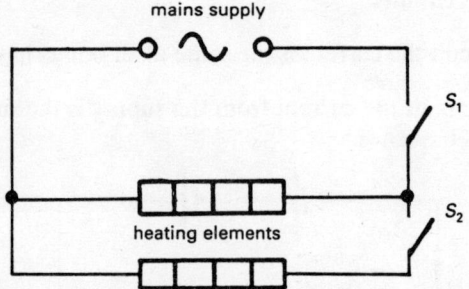

Closing switch S_1 allows one bar to be connected in series with the supply and switched on. When switches S_1 and S_2 are closed, both bars of the fire are switched on and connected in parallel with the supply.

6. *A car lighting circuit can be represented by the following circuit diagram.*

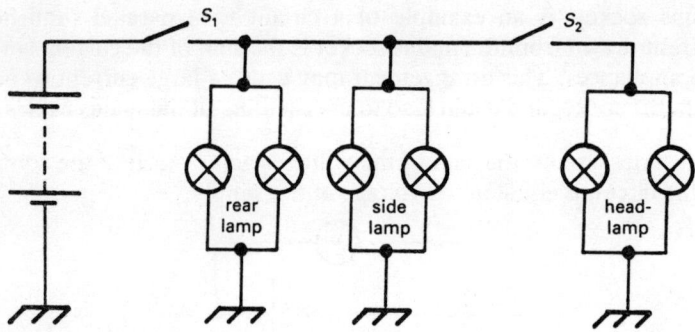

The car body acts as part of the circuit. In the diagram above the body of the car is denoted by the symbol ⊥⊥ . *Therefore, there is a complete circuit for each lamp in the diagram.*

In this circuit the rear and side lamps are switched on by closing switch S_1. The headlamps are operated by closing both switches, S_1 and S_2.

42

7. *Carry out calculations to find the resistance of circuits. To do the calculation you will have to remember and apply two relationships. The relationships are as follows.*

$$R_s = R_1 + R_2 + ...$$

$$\frac{1}{R_p} = \frac{1}{R_1} + \frac{1}{R_2} + ...$$

An example of the kind of calculating that might be expected of you is as follows.

What is the resistance of circuit 1 and circuit 2 shown below?

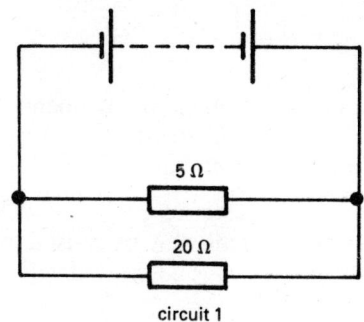

circuit 1

circuit 2

circuit 1 is a parallel circuit

$$\frac{1}{R_p} = \frac{1}{R_1} + \frac{1}{R_2}$$

$$= \frac{1}{5} + \frac{1}{20}$$

$$= \frac{5}{20}$$

$R_p = 4 \ ohms$

resistance of circuit 1 = 4 Ω

circuit 2 is a series circuit

$$R_s = R_1 + R_2$$

$$= 5 + 20$$

$$= 25 \ ohms$$

resistance of circuit = 25 Ω

Fault finding circuit

8. A simple continuity tester can be made using a battery, bulb and some wire. These are connected in a circuit as follows.

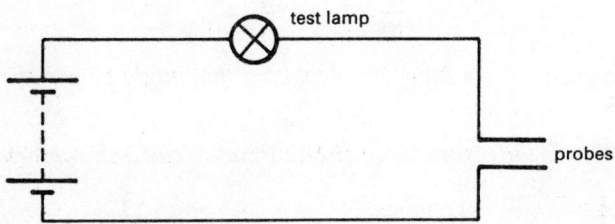

The tester can be used to detect whether part of a circuit is open or shorted. An open circuit is where there is a gap in the circuit where a gap should not be. For example, a blown bulb is an open circuit.

A short circuit is where there is a very low resistance path round a component in the circuit. The very low resistance path may be caused by touching wires. For example, the piece of wire which is connected across the bulb, as shown below, short circuits the bulb.

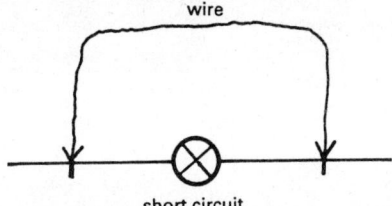

Suppose part of a circuit is open. When the tester is connected across that part the test lamp will not light.

If the part of the circuit under test is shorted, then, when the tester is connected across that part, the test lamp will have its normal brightness.

A rough check on whether part of a circuit has the expected resistance can be carried out using the tester. In this check the test lamp will glow dimly depending on the resistance of the circuit being checked.

More accurate checks on resistance would require the use of an ohmmeter. The ohmmeter is used in a similar way to the tester. It gives a reading of the resistance of the circuit.

SECTION 5: BEHIND THE WALL

Mains supply

1. Household appliances are connected in parallel across the mains supply.

Ring circuit

2. *The mains sockets in the home are wired in a special kind of parallel circuit called a ring circuit.*

   The ring circuit uses cable which has three wires — live (L), neutral (N) and earth (E). The live and neutral wires are connected to terminals behind the bottom two holes in each socket. The earth wire is connected to a terminal behind the top hole of each socket. Each wire forms a ring which starts from and finishes at the mains fuse box as shown in the diagram below.

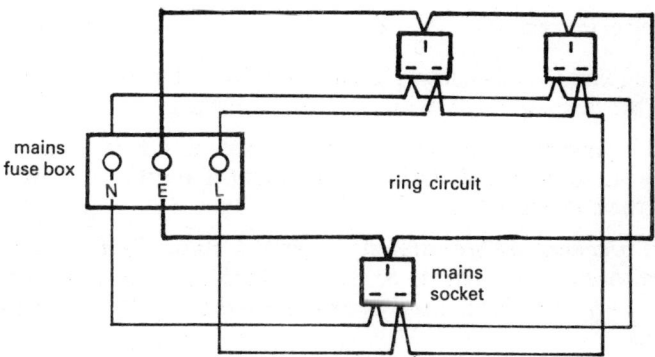

   The design of the ring circuit allows current to reach a socket by two routes. The wire for each route, therefore, only has to carry half the current which is drawn by the appliance connected to the socket.

3. *An advantage of the ring circuit over a normal parallel circuit is that its special design allows lighter, thinner, and therefore less expensive cable to be safely used for connecting sockets to the mains supply.*

Lighting circuit

4. *The circuit which is used for lighting is different from the ring circuit in a number of ways.*

45

For example, the lighting circuit, unlike the ring circuit, is a normal parallel circuit. A lighting circuit is shown in the diagram below.

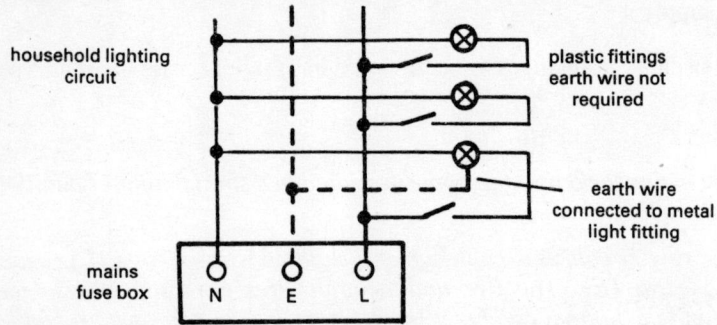

Also the current drawn by the lighting circuit is much less than that in the ring circuit. The cable which is used for the lighting circuit is, therefore, much thinner than that used for the ring circuit.

Fuses and circuit breakers

5. The ring circuit and lighting circuit are protected by fuses. Sometimes circuit breakers are used in place of the mains fuses.

    Circuit breakers are devices which act like an automatic switch. They quickly sense when the current in a circuit is too big and automatically switch the current off.

    Circuit breakers are sometimes preferred to fuses because they offer the convenience of being able to be reset by the push of a button after the fault has been cleared. Fuses need to be removed to have the blown fuse wire replaced.

Metering energy

6. The energy supplied to the ring circuit and lighting circuit is metered and is measured in kilowatt-hours. The kilowatt-hour is a unit of energy.

    The number of joules which is equivalent to a kilowatt-hour can be calculated as follows.

    1 kWh is the energy transferred by an appliance rated at 1 kW and switched on for 1 hour.

$$energy\ transferred = power \times time$$
$$1\ kWh = 1000 \times (60 \times 60)$$
$$= 3\ 600\ 000\ J$$

SECTION 6:   MOVEMENT FROM ELECTRICITY

Magnetic effect

1.   A current in a wire produces a magnetic field around the wire.

2.   When there is a current in a wire and the wire is placed in a magnetic field, a force acts on the wire.

   The direction of the force on the current-carrying wire depends on the direction of the current in the wire. It also depends on the direction of the magnetic field in which the wire is placed.

3.   An electromagnet is one example of a device where use is made of the magnetic effect of an electric current.

   Another device which makes use of the magnetic effect of a current is the electric motor.

Electric motor

4.   Make sure that you can identify the rotating coil, magnet, brushes and commutator on a simple diagram of an electric motor, such as that shown below.

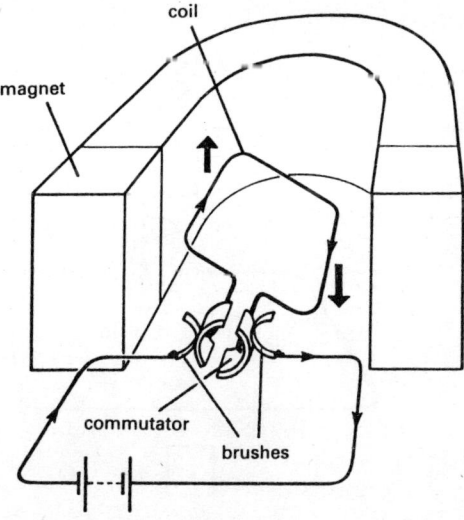

5. *The rotation of the coil in an electric motor can be explained as follows, using diagrams A, B and C below.*

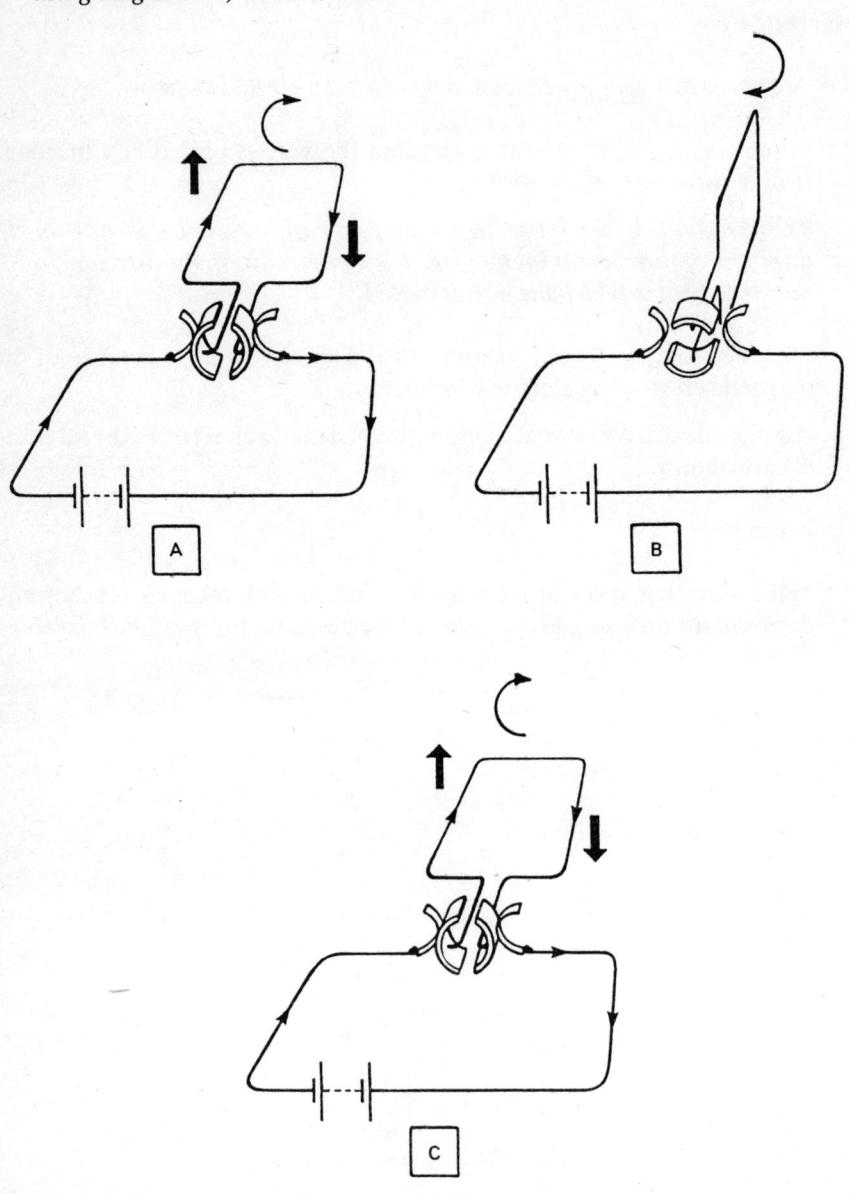

When the coil is in the flat position, as shown in diagram A, the commutator makes contact with the brushes and a current is supplied to the coil. The current in one side of the coil is in the opposite direction from the current in the other side. The magnetic field of the magnet and the current in the coil cause forces to act on the coil. An upwards force acts on one side of the coil and a downwards force acts on the other side of the coil.

This combination of forces acting on the coil makes it rotate into a vertical position as shown in diagram B. At this point, the commutator loses contact with the brushes and there is no current in the coil. The coil is able to rotate freely beyond the vertical position.

The commutator then makes contact with the brushes again as shown in diagram C. A current is again supplied to the coil. The combination of forces act on the coil in the same direction as before. The coil rotates to the vertical position. Contact is again momentarily lost. The coil continues to rotate, contact is made again with the brushes, current is then supplied to the coil, forces act and so on.

6. *Real motors operate by the same principles which apply to a simple laboratory model. However, the design of a real motor is slightly different. The brushes, for example, are made of carbon and are spring loaded. This arrangement makes for good electrical contact, reduces wear on the commutator and allows the coil to rotate freely.*

    The commutator is made up of many pairs of segments and coils are connected across each pair. The coils have many windings. This arrangement allows for a smoother rotation.

    The magnetic field is supplied by coils carrying an electrical current (called field coils) rather than a permanent magnet. The use of field coils enables the motor to be operated using alternating current.

UNIT 3 — HEALTH PHYSICS

The table below lists the sections and content of the Unit on Health Physics.

Section	Content
1. Use of thermometers in medicine	Types of thermometer
	Measuring body temperature
2. Using sound in medicine	Stethoscope
	Ultrasonic scanning
	Noise pollution
3. Light and sight	Refraction of light
	Image formation by the lens of the eye
	Short sight and long sight
	Spectacle lenses
	Fibre optics in medicine
4. Using the spectrum	Use of lasers in medicine
	Use of X-rays in medicine
	Use of ultraviolet and infrared radiation in medicine
5. Nuclear radiation — humans and medicine	Use of radioactivity in medicine
	Properties of radioactivity
	Activity
	Safety and radiation dose

The paragraphs in italics describe the additional knowledge which is needed for the Credit Level examination.

SECTION 1:   USE OF THERMOMETERS IN MEDICINE

Types of thermometer

1. Thermometers use materials which have a property, e.g., length, shape or colour, that changes with temperature in some way. The change in the property of the material is a measure of the temperature.

    A common type of thermometer uses a column of liquid, such as mercury or alcohol, contained in a narrow glass tube as shown in the diagram.

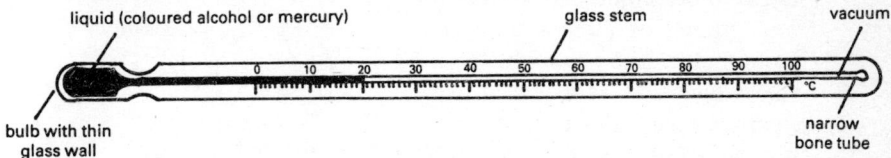

    The length of the liquid column changes as temperature increases. The length of the column of liquid in the tube is taken as a measure of the temperature of the thermometer's surroundings.

    A scale of temperature is marked on the glass tube. A common scale is the Celsius scale. The zero on this scale corresponds to the melting point of ice. The scale is given 100 divisions. The point marked 100 degrees celsius on the scale is made to correspond to the boiling point of water.

2. Most liquid in glass thermometers, such as common mercury thermometers, are able to measure a temperature range from –10 degrees celsius to 110 degrees celsius. A clinical thermometer is another example of a liquid in glass thermometer.

    The clinical thermometer is different in a number of respects from the common mercury thermometer. For example, the clinical thermometer is designed to read body temperature., It therefore has a range of only a few celsius degrees — from 35 degrees celsius to 42 degrees celsius.

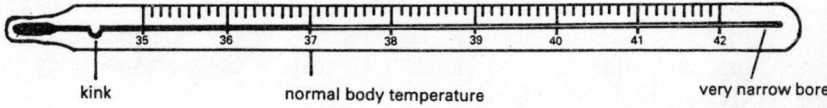

51

Another difference is that the clinical thermometer has a smaller bulb and a much narrower mercury column. This makes the clinical thermometer sensitive to small changes in temperature.

The clinical thermometer also has a narrow kink in the tube above the bulb as shown in the previous diagram. When the thermometer is removed from the body, the mercury starts to contract. The kink in the tube causes the mercury thread to break away from the mercury in the bulb. A column of mercury is therefore left above the kink. This allows time for the temperature to be read accurately even when the thermometer is not in contact with the body.

The shape of the glass tube of a clinical thermometer is different from that of the common thermometer. The glass tube has a bulge which acts as a lens which magnifies the mercury thread. This makes it easier to see the narrow thread against the scale and read the temperature.

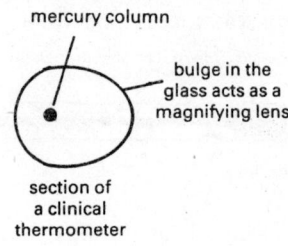

mercury column

bulge in the glass acts as a magnifying lens

section of a clinical thermometer

Measuring body temperature

3. Before making a measurement of body temperature, the clinical thermometer should be shaken to ensure that the mercury thread is joined up with the mercury in the bulb. The thermometer is then sterilised before placing it in the mouth.

Nature has arranged that the human body operates most efficiently at a temperature of 37 degrees celsius. Body temperatures which are different by a few degrees either side of this value confirm that a person has an illness.

High body temperatures indicate that the body is producing too much heat and cannot get rid of it quickly enough. Low body temperatures, on the other hand, indicate that the body is losing heat too quickly.

Knowledge of whether a person's temperature is high or low can help a doctor to make a diagnosis. The doctor can then decide on the best course of action to take in order to restore the person's body to its normal working condition.

SECTION 2:   USING SOUND IN MEDICINE

Stethoscope

1. Sound cannot be transmitted in a vacuum. Sound needs a medium, i.e. a solid, liquid or gas, to enable it to be transmitted.

2. A stethoscope is a kind of hearing aid used by doctors to listen to sounds from the internal organs of the body.

    Sound from the patient's body is collected by the stethoscope and transmitted through a column of air in a flexible tube to the ear of the listener. Two bell-shaped cavities, one open and one covered by a diaphragm, are connected to the end of the tube. Sounds from the patient's body are collected by the bell cavities. The bell cavity amplifies the sound in much the same way as the hollow body of a guitar.

    The open bell is pressed against the skin when listening to low frequency sounds such as those from the heart. The closed bell can amplify the higher frequency sounds better and is used when listening to sounds from the lungs.

Ultrasonic scanning

3. High frequency vibrations beyond the range of human hearing, i.e. above 20 000 hertz, are called ultrasound. Ultrasound is used in medicine. One use for ultrasound is in monitoring the development of a baby in its mother's womb.

4. *Ultrasound, although it cannot be heard, produces echoes in the same way as audible sound frequencies. Echoes are produced when ultrasound travels through the body and passes from one type of body tissue to another.*

    The data provided by measuring the strength of the different echoes can be processed by a computer. The information from the processed data is used to enable an image of the inside of part of a person's body to be displayed on a TV monitor.

Noise pollution

5. Noise from traffic in a busy city may be considered as a pollution of the environment. Excessively loud music from radios and hi-fi equipment

may be considered an annoyance and a pollutant. Legal limits are set for the amount of noise pollution we are expected to tolerate.

6. Exposure to high levels of noise over a period of time could result in damage to hearing.

    Sound levels are measured in decibels.

    Silence is recorded as 0 decibels.

    The ticking of a watch is around 30 decibels.

    60 decibels is a tolerable sound level. This value represents the sound level at your ear drums during normal conversation.

    100 decibels of sound, however, could not be tolerated for long without protection for your ears. This represents the sound level which could be produced at your ears when you are a few metres from a pheumatic drill.

    A sound level of 120 decibels can occur in a disco when you are about 1 metre from the loudspeakers.

SECTION 3: LIGHT AND SIGHT

Refraction of light

1. When a ray of light passes from one material to another, its path can undergo a change of direction. This change in direction is called refraction.

    Light travelling from air to glass is refracted. The path of the light is bent towards a line drawn perpendicular to the glass surface as shown by the diagram.

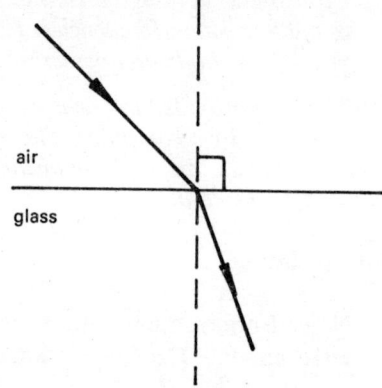

In travelling from glass to air, the ray of light is refracted away from the line perpendicular to the surface as shown.

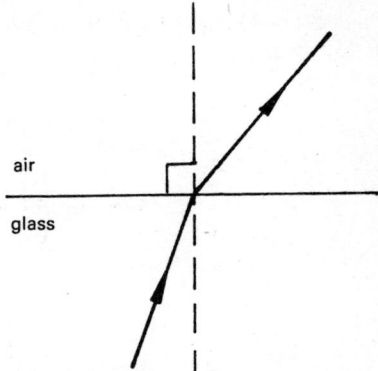

At Credit Level, you should be able to use correctly the terms angle of incidence, angle of refraction and normal. For example, you would be expected to label correctly a diagram such as that shown.

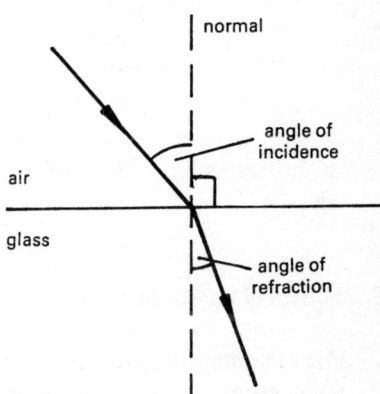

2. Convex and concave lenses refract light which is parallel to the axes of the lenses as shown below.

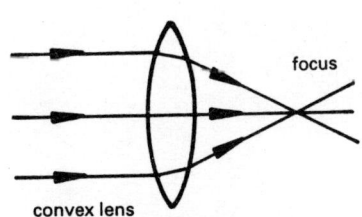

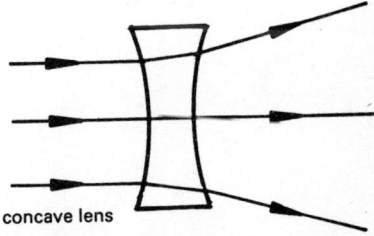

The curvature of the lens affects the refraction of the light as shown in the diagram.

A fat convex lens, i.e. one with a large curvature, refracts light more than a thin lens.

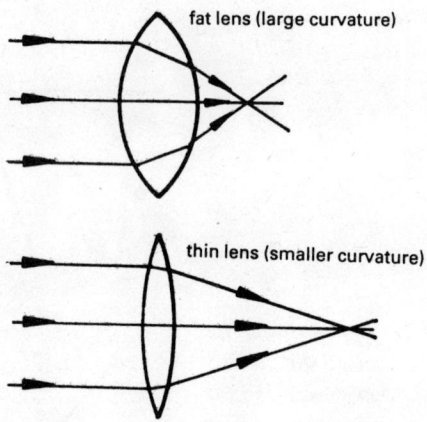

In the fatter lens, the rays of light are brought to a focus closer to the lens.

3. The focal length of a convex lens can be measured as follows.

Place the lens in front of a screen fixed on a wall on the opposite side of a room from a window. Produce a sharp image of a bright distant object outside the window on the screen. Measure the distance between the lens and screen. This distance is the focal length of the lens.

Image formation by the lens of the eye

4. The lens of the eye is a convex lens. It forms an image of an object by focusing light from each point of the object on to the retina. The image which is formed on the retina is upside down compared to the object. It is also laterally inverted, i.e. the left hand side of the object appears as the right hand side of the image.

5. The formation of the image on the retina can be explained using a ray diagram. Rays of light passing through a convex lens are refracted according to the following rules.

    A ray parallel to the axis of the lens is refracted through the focal point of the lens.

    A ray which is directed at the centre of the lens passes straight through the lens.

Drawing these two rays from a point on the object locates the position of the image of the point.

A ray diagram showing how an image is formed on the retina is given below.

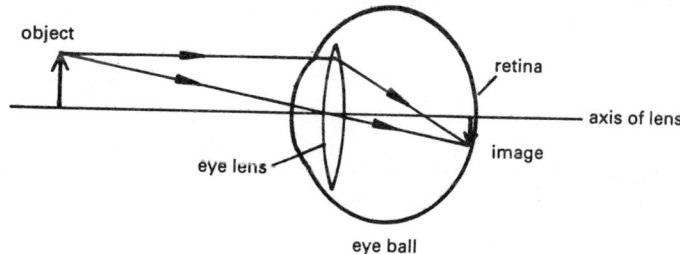

6. *The shape of the eye lens can be changed. Muscles in the eye can make the lens fat or thin.*

When a distant object is being viewed, the muscles are relaxed and the lens has a thin shape. When the object being viewed is close to the eye, the muscles make the lens fatter. This allows the lens to focus the rays from the object on to the retina and form a sharp image.

Ray diagrams showing the formation of images of distant and close up objects are given below.

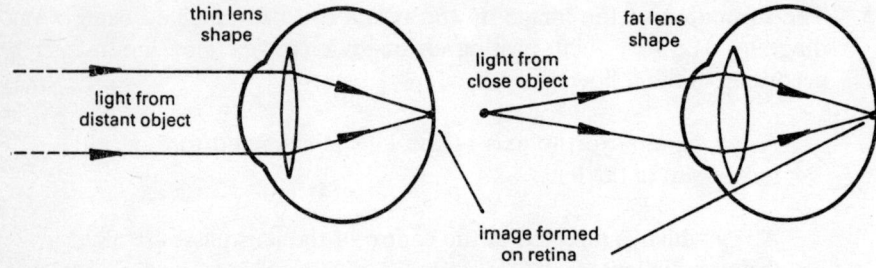

7. *Carry out calculations using the expression for the power of a lens. These calculations involve remembering the following relationship.*

$$power\ of\ a\ lens = \frac{1}{focal\ length}$$

Lens power is measured in dioptres (D) and focal length is measured in metres.

An example of the kind of calculating that might be expected of you is as follows.

A spectacle lens has a focal length of 40 cm. What is the power of the lens?

$$power\ of\ lens = \frac{1}{focal\ length}$$

$$= \frac{1}{0\cdot40}$$

$$= 2\cdot5\ dioptres$$

$$= 2\cdot5\ D$$

Short sight and long sight

8. Some people have an eye lens which is too fat (too big a curvature) and therefore too powerful for the size of the eyeball. Even when the muscles of the eye are relaxed the lens is still too fat and powerful. This means that light from distant objects is brought to a focus in front of the retina as shown in the diagram below.

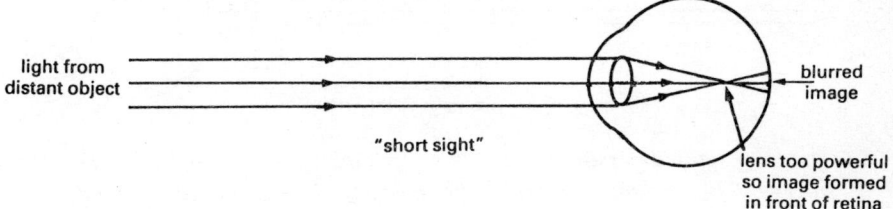

A blurred image is therefore formed.

Only objects which are viewed at a short distance from the eye can be seen clearly. This condition is known as short sight.

Other people have an eye lens which cannot be made fat and powerful enough for the size of the eyeball. This means that the light from an object which is viewed close to the eye cannot be focussed on to the retina as shown in the diagram below.

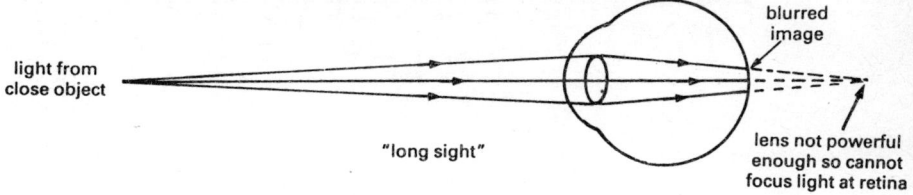

A blurred image is therefore formed.

Only objects which are a long distance from the eye can be seen clearly. This condition is known as long sight.

Spectacle lenses

9. Short sight and long sight can be corrected using spectacle lenses.

    In the short sight condition, the eye lens is too powerful to allow distant objects to be viewed clearly.

59

This condition is overcome by placing a concave lens in front of the eye lens. This has the effect of diverging the rays of light before they reach the eye lens. The eye lens can now focus the diverging rays so that they form a sharp image on the retina as shown below.

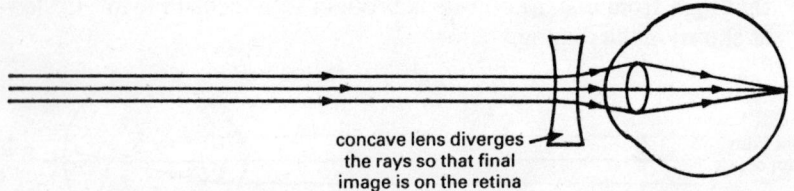

concave lens diverges
the rays so that final
image is on the retina

The long sighted person is not able to see clearly objects which are close to the eye. The eye lens is not powerful enough to focus the light from a close up object on to the retina.

This condition is overcome by placing a convex lens in front of the eye lens. This has the effect of converging the light rays before they reach the eye lens. The eye lens can now focus the converging rays to form a sharp image on the retina as shown below.

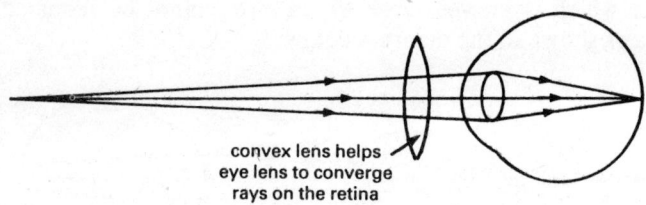

convex lens helps
eye lens to converge
rays on the retina

Fibre optics in medicine

10. Optical fibres are used in an endoscope. The endoscope is a medical tool which is used for transmitting light so that parts inside a person's body can be looked at.

    The part of the endoscope which goes into the person's body is not near the hot source which produces the light. The light reaching the inside parts of the body can, therefore, be thought of as 'cold light'.

    The optical fibres in the endoscope are designed to allow the light from the source to be transmitted through them. The light is transmitted through the fibre by the process of total internal reflection.

The light coming from the end of the optical fibre illuminates the inside of the body. Light is reflected from the part of body which is being viewed. The reflected light then travels back up another set of fibres to the viewing part of the endoscope where an image of the inside of the body is formed.

The diagram below shows the path of the light in an endoscope.

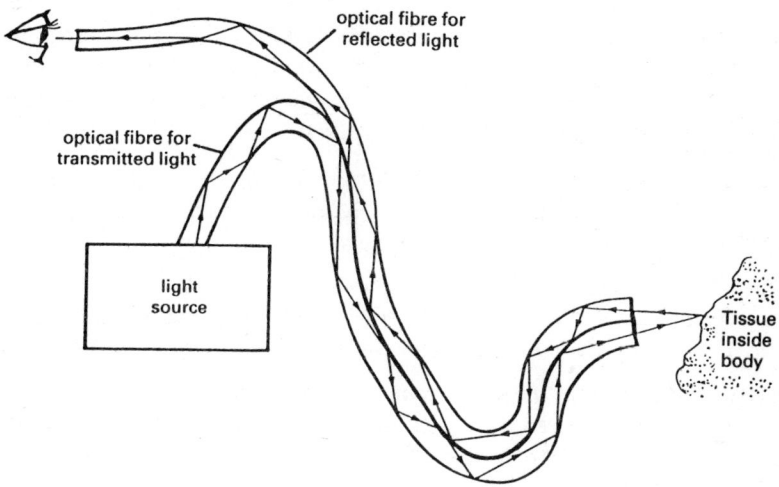

SECTION 4: USING THE SPECTRUM

Use of lasers in medicine

1. Lasers are used in medicine in a number of ways.

    One use which is made of the laser is in the removal of tumours. Surgery is difficult when the tumor is growing in places such as the brain or spinal column. In such cases, the laser can be used as a kind of scalpel. A fine beam of laser light can be directed at the affected tissue. The beam is able to vaporise the tumour without causing any damage to neighbouring healthy tissue.

Use of X-rays in medicine

2. X-rays can be detected using photographic film. X-rays are absorbed by different amounts depending on the type of body material they meet, e.g. bone and muscle tissue. An X-ray photograph is taken by placing a

photographic film behind part of the patient's body. X-rays are then directed at the body.

The X-rays which pass through the body expose the film by different amounts. In this way an image of the internal part of the body, e.g. a broken bone, is formed on the film.

3. *X-ray photographs are useful in medicine but they have their limitations. The target area is often hidden by other organs in the body and, therefore, the image on the X-ray film may not be clear. Computerised tomography is a technique which gets round this problem.*

   In this technique, an X-ray source directs a beam of X-rays at the patient. Detectors measure the amount of radiation which passes through the patient's body.

   The X-ray source is rotated and measurements of the radiation reaching the detectors are made for a number of positions round the patient's body. In this way, a section or slice of the patient's body is exposed to the X-rays.

   All of the data from the measurements made on the section of the patient's body are then processed by a computer. The processed data are used to produce an image of a section of the inside of the patient's body on a TV monitor.

   The advantage of computerised tomography is that it gives images which have more detail than those provided by ordinary X-ray photographs. Small tumours growing in the body can, therefore, be precisely located by this technique.

Use of ultraviolet and infrared radiation in medicine

4. Excessive exposure to ultraviolet radiation may produce skin cancer. However, a controlled amount of this radiation on the skin can be beneficial. Skin disorders such as acne can be treated by controlled exposure to ultraviolet radiation.

   Infrared radiation, when absorbed by body tissue, causes the tissue to heat up. The heating effect of the radiation is used in the treatment of damaged muscles. The heat increases the flow of blood to the damaged tissue and speeds up the healing process.

Infrared radiation can also be used to detect the presence of unhealthy tissue in a patient's body. Unhealthy tissue is warmer than normal tissue. A special kind of photograph can be taken using the infrared radiation which is emitted by the patient's body. The special infrared photograph, called a thermogram, identifies areas of different temperature. The areas of different temperature show up as areas of different colour on the thermogram. The thermogram can help a diagnosis to be made of the patient's condition.

SECTION 5:   NUCLEAR RADIATION — HUMANS AND MEDICINE

Use of radioactivity in medicine

1. Radiation from radioactive sources can destroy living cells or change the way in which cells develop.

    Radiation, however, has beneficial effects. Radiation from a radioactive source can be directed at cancer cells in a person's body. The radiation destroys the cancer cells.

2. Even small amounts of radiation can be easily detected.

    Use is made of this in examining whether parts of the body, e.g. kidneys and lungs, are functioning properly.

    A small amount of radioactive material is injected into the body so that it travels to the organ which is to be examined. The amount of radiation coming from the organ is detected and measured. Measurements are processed by a computer and an image of the organ is displayed on a TV monitor. This can enable a diagnosis to be made.

Properties of radioactivity

3. An atom is made up of a small nucleus surrounded by orbiting electrons. The nucleus of the atom contains particles called protons and neutrons.

    The nuclei of some atoms emit radiation. The radiation is of three types — alpha particles, beta particles and gamma rays. The three radiations transfer energy from the nucleus when they are emitted.

4. The energy associated with each of the three radiations is absorbed by the material through which the radiation passes. The amount of energy which is absorbed depends on the type of radiation and the nature of the absorbing material.

Alpha radiation transfers more energy to an absorber than beta or gamma radiation. Thus the range of the alpha radiation in an absorbing material is less than that of beta or gamma. Alpha radiation is absorbed by the thickness of the skin or by a few centimetres of air.

Beta radiation is more penetrating. It can pass through the skin, but it is absorbed by a few centimetres of body tissue or a few millimetres of aluminium.

Gamma radiation is the most penetrating. It can easily penetrate body tissue. It requires a few centimetres of lead or about 1 metre of concrete to absorb it.

5. When radiation passes through an absorbing material it transfers energy to the material.

The means by which the radiation transfers energy to the absorbing material is called ionisation. Ionisation involves electrons being torn from atoms in the absorbing material.

For a given thickness of absorber, alpha radiation produces most ionisation, beta next and gamma least.

When alpha particles, beta particles or gamma rays collide with the atoms of an absorbing material, two types of charged particles are produced. These are positively charged atoms and negatively charged electrons. These charged particles are referred to as ions. The charged atom is a positive ion and the negatively charged electron is a negative ion.

6. *The ionising effect of radiation is used as one way of detecting radiation. The ionising effect is used by the Geiger-Muller (GM) tube in detecting radiation.*

The GM tube is a hollow cylinder filled with a gas at low pressure. There is a central electrode inside the GM tube and the tube has a mica window at one end. A voltage supply is connected across the casing of the tube and the central electrode as shown in the following diagram.

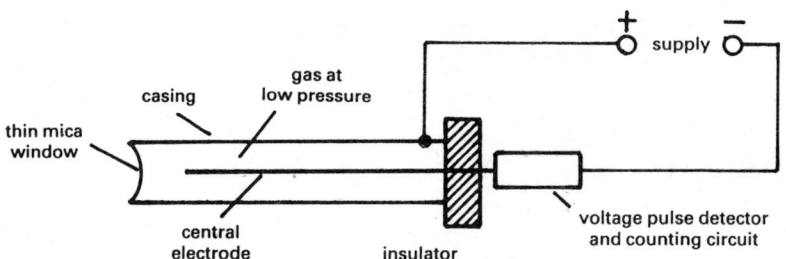

When radiation enters the tube it produces ions in the gas. The ions cause the gas in the tube to conduct and a current is produced in the tube for a short time. The current produces a voltage pulse. The pulse is amplified and counted. Each voltage pulse which is counted corresponds to one ionising radiation entering the GM tube.

Activity

7. The activity of a radioactive source is the number of ionising radiations it emits per second. Activity is measured in becquerels. One becquerel is one ionising radiation emitted per second, i.e. an alpha particle, a beta particle or a gamma ray emitted per second.

8. The activity of a radioactive source decreases with time.

    The time taken for the activity of a radioactive source to reduce by half is called the 'half-life' of the source.

    The half-life of a radioactive source can be measured as follows.

    Radiation from the source is detected by a GM tube. The activity of the source is measured at fixed intervals of time. Account is taken of the background radiation in making this measurement. A graph of activity of the source against time is plotted. From the graph, the time taken for activity to fall by half is calculated. An average of a number of values obtained from the graph are calculated. The average is taken as a measurement of the half-life of the radioactive source.

9. *Carry out calculations to find the half-life of a radioactive source. The type of calculating that might be expected of you is as follows.*

   A radioactive source has a half-life of 20 minutes. At a particular time the activity of the source is 3000 becquerels. What is the activity of the source 1 hour later?

   1 hour = 60 minutes
   60 minutes represents 3 × 20 minutes = 3 half-lives

   $$activity\ of\ source = 3000 \times \frac{1}{2} \times \frac{1}{2} \times \frac{1}{2}$$
   $$= 375\ Bq$$

Safety and radiation dose

10. Safety precautions are necessary when working with radioactive sources. Radioactive sources should be kept away from the body and never brought close to the eyes. Sources should be shielded from the body and handled using tongs and other lifting tools. Exposure to radiation is monitored using film badges to ensure that the radiation dose received by the person does not exceed safety limits.

The amount of radiation received by body tissue depends on the type and energy of the radiation to which the tissue has been exposed. The amount of radiation received will depend, for example, on whether the radiation is alpha, beta, gamma or some other radiation.

A way of expressing the radiation dose received from different sources is in terms of a quantity called 'dose equivalent'. Dose equivalent is measured in sieverts. Thus a dose of one sievert from an alpha radiation source, for example, is equivalent to a dose of one sievert from a beta radiation source or any other source of radiation.

The risk of damage to body tissue from a dose of radiation depends on the size of the dose. The risk of damage also depends on the type of body tissue absorbing the radiation. Some tissues of the body are more susceptible to harm from radiation than others. This is taken into account when estimating the dose of radiation a person has effectively received.

UNIT 4 — ELECTRONICS

The table below lists the sections and content of the Unit on Electronics.

Section	Content
1. Electronic systems	Input, process and output
	Digital and analogue signals
2. Output devices	Output devices producing light, sound and movement
	The light emitting diode
	Seven-segment display
3. Input devices	Microphone, thermocouple, solar cell
	Thermistor and light dependent resistor
	Switch, capacitor and voltage divider
	Selecting input devices for given applications
4. Digital processes	Transistor as a switch
	Simple switching circuits using transistors; fire alarm, burglar alarm, parking light, time delay
	Digital logic gates
	Using logic gates for automation and control
	Clock signals
	Counter
5. Analogue processes	Devices containing amplifiers
	Amplifier gain

The paragraphs in italics describe the additional knowledge which is needed for the Credit Level examination.

SECTION 1:   ELECTRONIC SYSTEMS

Input, process and output

1. It is useful to think of an electronic system as consisting of three parts — input, process and output. The system can be represented by a diagram as shown below.

The input section is where an electrical signal is produced. In the middle section, the input signal is changed and processed in some way. In the output part, the processed signal is used to operate some sort of output device, e.g., loudspeaker, lamp, buzzer.

Digital and analogue signals

2. The signal from the output part of an electronic system can be in a digital or an analogue form.

In a digital signal the output is either high or low, there is no in-between value. In an analogue signal, the output varies in a continuous way and can have any in-between value.

You should be able to identify signals as either analogue or digital when they are displayed on the screen of an oscilloscope.

For example, it is expected that you would recognise the waveform shown in the diagram below as representing a digital output. The pattern has the high-low, on-off characteristics of a digital signal.

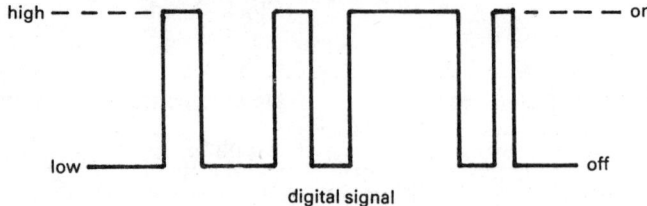

digital signal

68

The following diagram has a pattern which varies in a continuous way. You should be able to recognise this is representing an analogue signal.

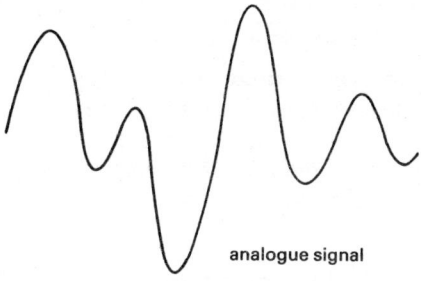

analogue signal

SECTION 2:   OUTPUT DEVICES

Output devices producing light, sound, movement

1. Output devices can convert the electrical signals produced by an electronic system into either light or sound or movement. You should be able to give some examples of output devices and say whether they produce light or sound or movement. For example:

   a lamp or a light emitting diode is an output device which produces light from electrical signals;

   a loudspeaker or a buzzer is an output device which produces sound from electrical signals;

   a solenoid or an electric motor is an output device which produces movement from electrical signals.

2. Output devices can be labelled as digital or analogue. You are expected to be able to name some digital and analogue output devices. You might use the following as examples.

   A light emitting diode is cither in an on-state or an off-state. It is either one thing or the other, an 'on' or an 'off', with nothing in between. It is therefore a digital device.

   A solenoid is a device which is either on or off. It too is a digital device.

   A buzzer is either on or off. It is a digital device.

A loudspeaker, on the other hand, converts a continuously varying electrical audio signal into sound waves. It acts as an analogue device.

A lamp can also act as an analogue device since its brightness can be made to vary in a continuous way.

An electric motor can be used as an analogue output device since its speed can be made to vary in a continuous way.

3. *At Credit Level, you should be able to select the output device which is most suited to a given electronic system.*

   For example:

   a suitable output device for an electronic buggy would be the electric motor for driving the wheels;

   a suitable output device for an electronic traffic control system would be a lamp;

   a solenoid could be used as the output device for operating a signal arm;

   a light emitting diode could be used as an output device to show whether an electronic system was switched on or off.

The light emitting diode

4. The symbol for a light emitting diode (LED) is as follows.

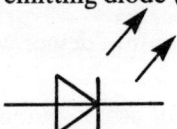

Make sure that you can recognise and draw the LED symbol.

5. The LED has a positive end and a negative end. The LED will produce light only if it is connected the right way round. A circuit diagram is given.

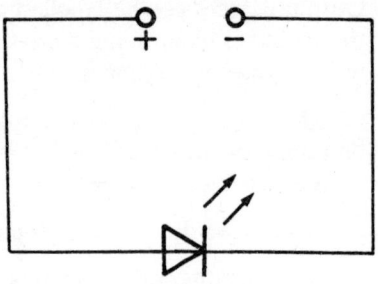

The positive end of the LED must be connected to the '+' terminal of the supply. The negative end of the LED must be connected to the '–' terminal.

6. The LED is normally connected in series with a resistor. The value of the
    resistor is chosen to ensure that the correct voltage and current are
    supplied to the LED.

    *For the Credit Level examination, you are expected to be able to draw a
    circuit which would allow a LED to light and operate at its correct rating.
    A suitable circuit diagram is given below.*

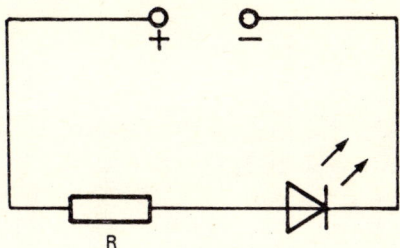

    *You should also be able to calculate the resistance of the series resistor
    which is used with the LED.*

    *An example of the kind of calculating that might be expected of you is as
    follows.*

    *A LED is connected in series with a resistor to a 5 V supply as
    shown in the diagram below.*

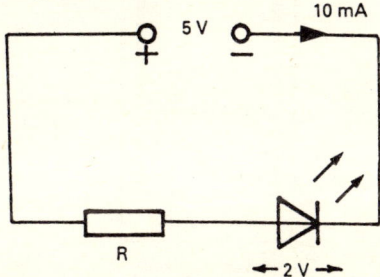

    *The voltage across the LED is 2 V and the current in it is 10 mA.
    What is the value of the series resistor?*

71

$$current\ in\ resistor\ (I) = current\ in\ LED$$
$$= 10\ mA$$

$$voltage\ across\ resistor = supply\ voltage - voltage\ across\ LED$$

$$voltage\ across\ resistor\ (V) = 5 - 2$$
$$= 3\ V$$

$$resistance\ of\ resistor\ (R) = \frac{V}{I}$$
$$= \frac{3}{10 \times 10^{-3}}$$
$$= 300\ \Omega$$

Seven-segment display

7.   Light emitting diodes are used in seven-segment displays. Seven light emitting diodes are used, one for each segment of the display. Numbers from 0 to 9 can be displayed by lighting up the appropriate light emitting diodes.

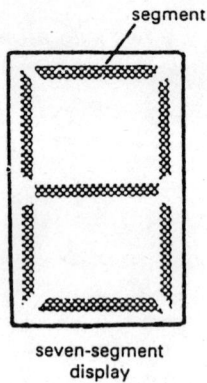

segment

seven-segment
display

8. *Light emitting diodes can also be used to display binary numbers. You should be able to calculate the decimal equivalent of a binary number in the range 0000 to 1001, (i.e. those binary numbers whose decimal equivalents are in the range 0 to 9).*

An example of the kind of calculating that might be expected of you is as follows.

What decimal number is represented by 0101?

$$0101 = (0 \times 8) + (1 \times 4) + (0 \times 2) + (1 \times 1)$$
$$= 0 + 4 + 0 + 1$$
$$= 5$$

SECTION 3:   INPUT DEVICES

Microphone, thermocouple, solar cell

1. Input devices are those which provide the input signal for an electronic system. The microphone, the thermocouple and the solar cell are examples of input devices.

   The microphone converts sound to electrical signals. The thermocouple converts heat to electrical signals. The solar cell converts light and infrared radiation into electrical signals.

Thermistor and light dependent resistor

2. The thermistor and the light dependent resistor (LDR) are also examples of input devices. These devices operate by changing their resistance and thereby the size of the electrical signal at the input.

   The resistance of the thermistor changes with temperature. The resistance of the LDR decreases as the intensity of the light on it increases.

3. Carry out calculations using $V = IR$ for a thermistor and a LDR.

   Examples of the kind of calculating that might be expected of you are as follows.

The resistance of a thermistor is 400 ohms when its temperature is 200 degrees celsius. The voltage across the thermistor is 4 volts. What is the current in the thermistor?

$$R = \frac{V}{I}$$

$$I = \frac{V}{R}$$

$$= \frac{4}{400}$$

$$= 0\cdot01 \text{ ampere}$$

current in thermistor $= 0\cdot01$ ampere

A light dependent resistor is connected to a 5 volt supply and placed in a darkened room. The current in the LDR is $0\cdot01$ amperes. What is the resistance of the LDR when it is in darkness?

$$R = \frac{V}{I}$$

$$= \frac{5}{0\cdot01}$$

$$= 500 \text{ ohms}$$

resistance of LDR = 500 ohms

Switch, capacitor and voltage divider

4. The switch, capacitor and voltage divider are further examples of devices which can be used to control the electrical signals at the input of an electronic system.

5. When a capacitor is being charged, as shown in the circuit below, the voltage across it increases with time.

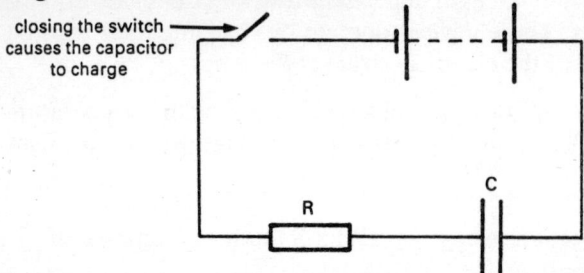

closing the switch
causes the capacitor
to charge

R

C

The time taken to charge the capacitor depends on the size of the capacitance of the capacitor and the resistance of the resistor.

74

6. *A voltage divider is an input device which divides up a voltage. An example of a voltage divider is a resistor connected in series with a variable resistor.*

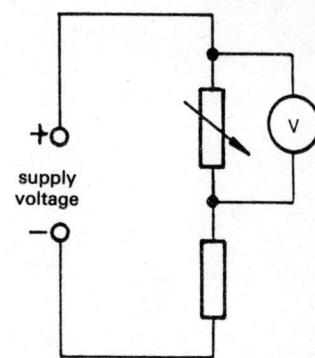

Adjusting the variable resistor divides up the voltage from the supply so that a fraction of it is developed across the variable resistor.

You should be able to carry out calculations involving circuits with voltage dividers.

An example of the kind of calculating that might be expected of you is as follows.

   A 2 kΩ resistor and a variable resistor are connected in series across a 5 V supply as shown on the following page.

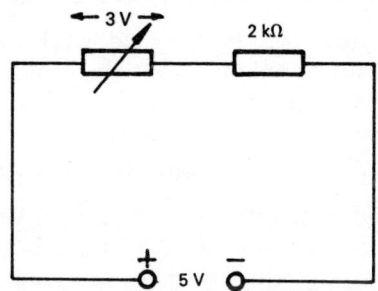

   The variable resistor is adjusted until 3 V is developed across it. Calculate the resistance of the variable resistor at this setting.

voltage of supply = sum of voltages across components

voltage across 2 kΩ resistor = 5 – 3 = 2 V

current in 2 kΩ resistor = $\dfrac{2}{2000}$ = 1 mA

current in variable resistor = 1 mA

resistance of variable resistor = $\dfrac{voltage}{current}$

$$= \frac{3}{1 \times 10^{-3}}$$

= 3000 Ω

Alternatively,

current in variable resistor equals current in resistor.

$$\frac{V_1}{R_1} = \frac{V_2}{R_2}$$

$$\frac{R_1}{R_2} = \frac{V_1}{V_2}$$

$$\frac{R_1}{2000} = \frac{3}{2}$$

$$R_1 = 3000 \ \Omega$$

Selecting input devices for given applications

7. At General Level, you are expected to be able to select from a list a suitable input device for a given application.

    An example of an application which you could be given is as follows.

    An electronic circuit is to be designed which will act as a time delay for the courtesy light in a car. The light is to be switched off after it has been on for a certain amount of time. Which of the following would be a suitable input device for the circuit?

    capacitor; thermocouple; voltage divider; switch

    The capacitor should be selected from the list. You should already know that when a capacitor is being charged, the voltage across it increases with time. The time delay circuit could be designed to switch off the light when the voltage across the capacitor reaches a certain value.

8. *At Credit Level, you are expected to be able to select an appropriate input device without having access to a list.*

    An example of the kind of selecting that might be expected of you is as follows.

    Name a suitable input device which could be used in an electronic thermometer.

    For this application, either a thermocouple or a thermistor would be selected since both of these input devices have properties which depend on temperature.

SECTION 4:   DIGITAL PROCESSES

Transistor as a switch

1. A transistor can be used in an electronic circuit to act like a switch.

    When the transistor conducts, it behaves like a closed switch. It provides
    a conducting path — the transistor is 'switched on'. When the transistor
    is not conducting it acts like an open switch — the transistor is in the
    'switched off' position.

Simple switching circuits which use transistors: fire alarm, burglar alarm, parking light, time delay

2. Make sure that you can recognise
    and draw this symbol for a
    transistor.

    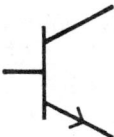

    In addition, make sure that you can identify from a circuit diagram the
    purpose of a simple transistor switching circuit. The circuit might act as a
    simple fire alarm, a burglar alarm, an automatic parking light, or as a
    simple time delay for switching on a LED.

    An example of the kind of circuit diagram which you might be presented
    with is as follows.

    Suggest a use for the following circuit.

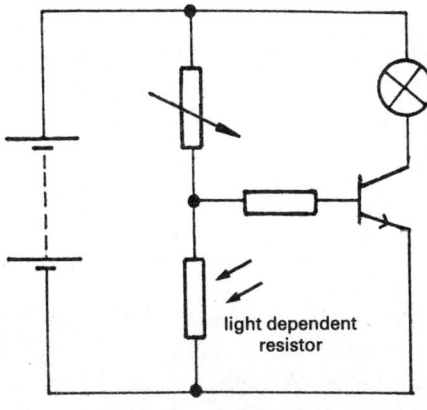

light dependent
resistor

You should identify this circuit as an automatic parking light. You should have recognised the LDR as the input device for this circuit. The LDR reacts to light and therefore would be suited to an automatic parking light. A simple burglar alarm is another possible use for the circuit.

3. *At Credit Level, you would be expected to be able to explain how simple transistor switching circuits work.*

   An example of the kind of explanation that might be expected of you is as follows.

   This circuit is used to act as a time delay. The LED lights up a few seconds after the switch is closed.

   Explain how the circuit works.

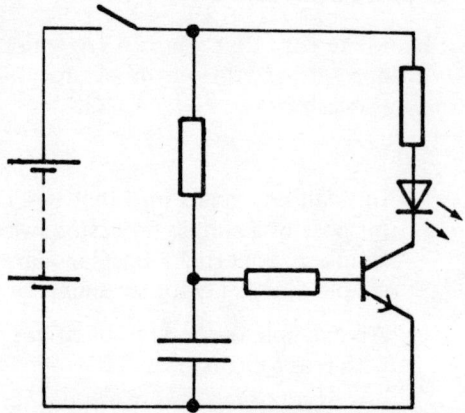

When the switch is closed, the capacitor starts to charge up and the voltage across the capacitor increases. After a few seconds, the voltage across the capacitor is high enough to switch on the transistor and make it conduct. The time taken for this to happen depends on the values of the resistance and the capacitance of the circuit. When the transistor starts to conduct, it acts like a closed switch. The LED now forms part of a complete circuit and it lights up.

Digital logic gates

4. A digital logic gate is an electronic circuit which allows a voltage to appear at its output when certain combinations of high and low voltages are applied at its input. A high voltage is sometimes referred to as 'logic 1'. A low voltage is sometimes called 'logic 0'.

78

5. Digital logic gates can have one or more inputs.

    A two-input AND gate, a two-input OR gate and a NOT gate are represented by the following symbols.

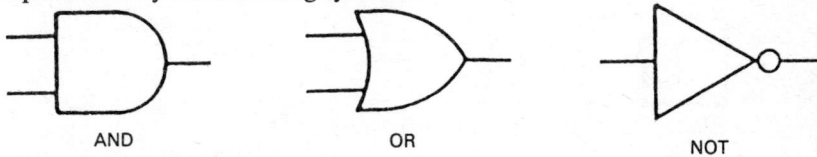

| AND | OR | NOT |

Make sure that you can recognise and draw each of these symbols.

6. A table called a 'truth table' can be used to show the output of a logic gate for all possible combinations of inputs.

    You should be able to draw the truth tables for the AND, OR and NOT gates described above. The truth table for each of the gates is as follows.

INPUT		OUTPUT
A	B	Z
0	0	0
0	1	0
1	0	0
1	1	1

AND

INPUT		OUTPUT
A	B	Z
0	0	0
0	1	1
1	0	1
1	1	1

OR

INPUT	OUTPUT
A	Z
0	1
1	0

NOT

At Credit Level, you are expected to be able to name the gate which belongs to a given truth table.

Using logic gates for automation and control

7. Digital logic gates can be combined and used in a number of simple situations for automation and control. You are expected to be able to explain how combinations of logic gates could be used in simple applications.

    An example of a simple application that you might be expected to explain is as follows.

    Explain how you would use logic gates to ensure that when a car's ignition is not switched on and its lights are switched on, a warning buzzer sounds.

The important words for this control application are 'ignition NOT switched on' and 'AND lights switched on'. A combination of a NOT gate and a two-input AND gate is therefore needed. The gates should be connected as shown below.

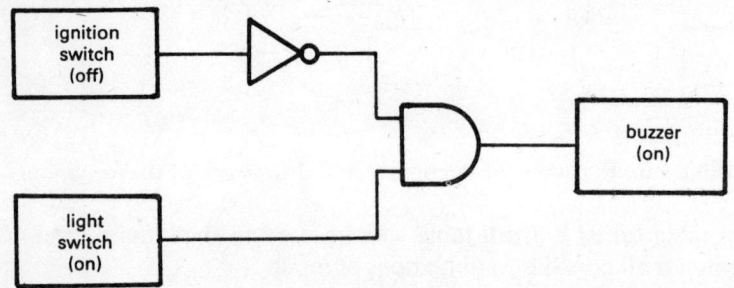

8. *At Credit Level, it is expected that you should be able to complete a truth table for a simple combination of logic gates.*

    An example of the kind of simple situation that you might have to deal with at Credit Level is as follows.

    Complete the truth table given below for the following combination of gates.

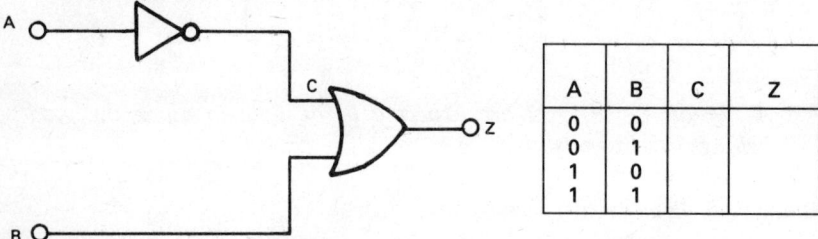

A	B	C	Z
0	0		
0	1		
1	0		
1	1		

The completed table is as follows.

A	B	C	Z
0	0	1	1
0	1	1	1
1	0	0	0
1	1	0	1

Clock signals

9. A digital circuit can be assembled to produce a regular sequence of voltage pulses. The circuit acts like a clock. However, instead of ticks and tocks, the clock produces high and low voltage pulses.

A simple oscillator circuit which produces clock pulses can be assembled using a resistor, capacitor and NOT gate as shown in the diagram below.

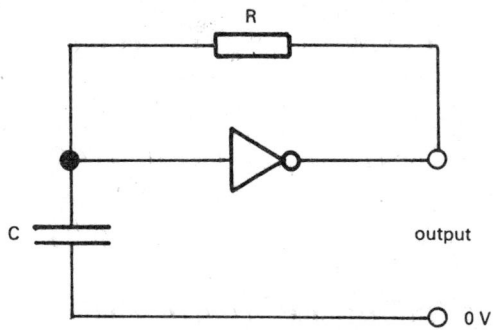

The way in which this oscillator works can be explained as follows.

At the start the capacitor is about to be charged up. At this point, the output of the NOT gate is high. The capacitor starts to charge up and the voltage across it rises to a high.

This high voltage at the input of the NOT gate makes its output go low. The capacitor now discharges through the resistor.

As the capacitor discharges, the voltage across it becomes low. This causes the input voltage to the NOT gate to become low.

The voltage at the output of the NOT gate then becomes high. The capacitor starts to charge up again and so the oscillation continues.

The frequency of oscillation is controlled by the time taken for the capacitor to charge and the time taken for it to discharge. The frequency of the clock pulses therefore depends on the size of the capacitance and resistance of the circuit.

Counter

10. Digital circuits can be assembled which will count clock pulses. Counting circuits are used for a number of electronic devices. For example, a counting circuit is used in a digital watch.

    The counting circuits use binary notation for the counting process. The voltage output of the counter circuit represents a binary number.

    The output from the counter circuit can be converted to a decimal number using a binary decoder circuit as shown in the following diagram.

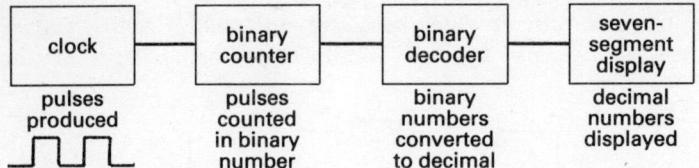

The output from the decoder circuit can be used to drive a seven-segment display on which the decimal number can be shown.

SECTION 5:   ANALOGUE PROCESS

Devices containing amplifiers

1. You should be able to identify from a list of devices those devices in which amplifiers play an important part.

   An example of a list which you might be presented with is as follows.

   Which of the devices in the list below have an amplifier?

   radio; torch; TV set; electric kettle; toaster; hearing aid

   You should recognise the radio, TV set and hearing aid as devices containing amplifiers.

2. The function of an amplifier in electronic systems such as radios, intercoms and music centres is to boost the strength of the electrical audio signal from the input part of the system.

3. An audio amplifier is designed so that its output signal is a larger copy of the input signal. The output signal of an audio amplifier has the same frequency, but a larger amplitude than the input signal.

Amplifier gain

4. Carry out calculations involving the input voltage, output voltage and voltage gain of an amplifier. In order to carry out the calculation, you will need to remember that the voltage gain of an amplifier is defined as follows.

$$\text{voltage gain} = \frac{\text{voltage output}}{\text{voltage input}}$$

An example of the kind of calculating that might be expected of you is as follows.

82

An amplifier has a voltage gain of 50. The output voltage from the amplifier is 10 volts. What voltage is supplied to the input of the amplifier?

$$\text{voltage gain} = \frac{\text{voltage output}}{\text{voltage input}}$$

$$\text{voltage input} = \frac{\text{voltage output}}{\text{voltage gain}}$$

$$= \frac{10}{50}$$

$$= 0 \cdot 2 \text{ volts}$$

5. *The voltage gain of an amplifier could be measured as follows.*

Use a signal generator to supply an alternating voltage to the input of the amplifier. Measure the peak input voltage using an oscilloscope. Connect the oscilloscope across the output of the amplifier. Measure the peak output voltage. Calculate $\dfrac{\text{voltage output}}{\text{voltage input}}$ *to find the value of the voltage gain of the amplifier.*

6. *The power delivered by an amplifier can be calculated using the expression* $\dfrac{V^2}{R}$ *where V is the output voltage and R is the resistance of the load which is connected across the output of the amplifier.*

7. *The power gain of an amplifier is the ratio of the power output to the power input.*

$$\text{power gain} = \frac{\text{power output}}{\text{power input}}$$

Carry out calculations using the above relationship for power gain.

An example of the kind of calculating that might be expected of you is as follows.

An amplifier delivers a power of 100 W. The power which is supplied to the amplifier is 0·5 W. What is the power gain of the amplifier?

$$\text{power gain} = \frac{\text{output power}}{\text{input power}}$$

$$= \frac{100}{0 \cdot 5}$$

$$= 200$$

UNIT 5 — TRANSPORT

The table below lists the sections and content of the Unit on Transport.

Section	Content
1. On the move	Average speed Instantaneous speed Speed and acceleration Speed-time graphs
2. Forces	Effects of force Measuring force Friction and movement Newton's First Law Newton's Second Law Seat belts and Newton's Laws
3. Movement means energy	Kinetic energy and gravitational potential energy Work and energy Conservation of energy

The paragraphs in italics describe the additional knowledge which is needed for the Credit Level examination.

SECTION 1:   ON THE MOVE

Average speed

1. The average speed of a body is defined as the distance travelled by an object divided by the time it takes to travel that distance.

$$\text{average speed} = \frac{\text{distance travelled}}{\text{time taken}}$$

One way of estimating the average speed of a body would be to use a measuring tape and a stopwatch. The distance to be travelled by the object would be measured with the tape. The time taken for the object to travel that distance would be measured by starting the stopwatch at the beginning of its travel and stopping the watch at the end. The average speed is then calculated by dividing the distance travelled by the time recorded on the stopwatch.

2. Carry out calculations using the following relationship.

$$\text{average speed} = \frac{\text{distance travelled}}{\text{time taken}}$$

An example of the kind of calculating that might be expected of you is as follows.

An athlete has an average speed of 8 metres per second during a race over 400 metres. How long did the athlete take to cover the distance?

$$\text{average speed} = \frac{\text{distance travelled}}{\text{time taken}}$$

$$\text{time taken} = \frac{\text{distance travelled}}{\text{average speed}}$$

$$= \frac{400}{8}$$

$$= 50 \text{ seconds}$$

Instantaneous speed

3. Rather than average speed, it may be more important to know the speed of an object at a particular instant of time during its journey. The object's speed at a particular instant is called the instantaneous speed of the object.

    Instantaneous speed can be measured by timing the object as it travels over a very small distance. The smaller the distance, the smaller will be the measured time and the better will be the estimate of the object's instantaneous speed at that point and time in its travel.

    Two light gates, a small measured distance apart, could be connected to an electronic timing circuit as shown.

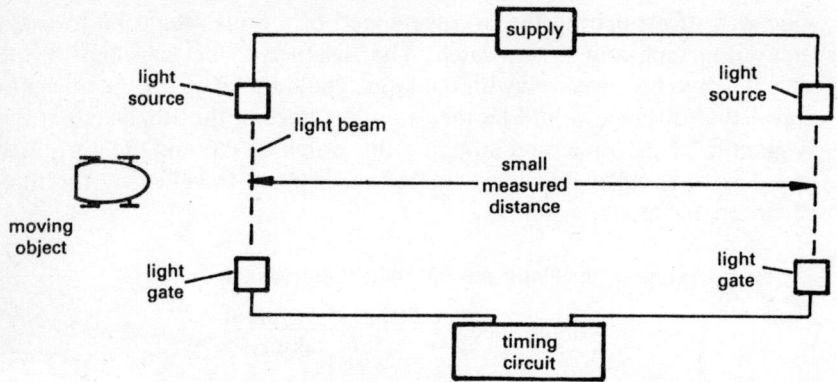

    As the object passes through the gates, it starts and stops the electronic timer. The instantaneous speed can be measured by dividing the measured distance by the time taken.

4. *The method which is used to measure the time of travel will have an effect on the accuracy of the estimate of the instantaneous speed.*

    For example, a hand-held stopwatch would not be appropriate. Human reaction time in starting and stopping the watch would cast much doubt on the accuracy of the measured time and, therefore, on the value for the instantaneous speed. Likewise, an electronic timer which recorded time in seconds would not be appropriate.

    In order to measure instantaneous speed, the time interval must be as short as possible. If this is not the case, the estimate being made is likely to be that of **average** *rather than* **instantaneous** *speed.*

86

5. *At Credit Level, you are expected to be able to give examples of situations where the instantaneous speed and average speed are different.*

   *The fact is, that for **most** situations, the value for instantaneous speed of an object and its average speed are normally different. This occurs in situations where the object's instantaneous speed is changing.*

   For example, consider a situation where the object is accelerating. The object's average speed must have a value somewhere between the maximum value of the instantaneous speed and the minimum value. In the situation where the acceleration happens to be uniform, the instantaneous speed of the body has a value equal to that of the average speed at only one point in time. At all other times, the instantaneous speed will have a different value from that of the average speed.

   In the situation where the instantaneous speed of an object throughout its journey remains the same, the value of the object's instantaneous speed will be the same as the object's average speed for the journey. This situation, however, is the exception rather than the rule. In most situations, for any given point in time, the instantaneous speed of a body will have a different value from that of the average speed.

Speed and acceleration

6. Speed (either instantaneous or average) is distance travelled per unit time. Speed is, therefore, measured in metres per second or kilometres per hour or miles per hour. Any unit of distance divided by a unit of time will give a unit of speed.

   When an object's speed changes with time, i.e. when it is speeding up or slowing down, the object is said to be accelerating or decelerating. Acceleration is defined as follows.

   $$\text{acceleration} = \frac{\text{change in speed}}{\text{time taken for change}}$$

   This definition means that the unit for acceleration will be unit of speed divided by unit of time. Acceleration can, therefore, be measured, for example, in metres per second divided by seconds, i.e. metres per second per second.

87

7. It is expected that you should be able to calculate the acceleration of an object.

An example of the kind of calculating that might be expected of you is as follows.

> A car is travelling along a motorway at 13 metres per second. The car's speed then increases steadily. After 3 seconds, the car is travelling at 22 metres per second. What is the acceleration of the car?
>
> $$\text{acceleration} = \frac{\text{change in speed}}{\text{time taken for change}}$$
>
> $$= \frac{22 - 13}{3}$$
>
> $$= \frac{9 \text{ metres per second}}{3 \text{ seconds}}$$
>
> $$= 3 \text{ metres per second per second}$$

Had the car's speed been expressed in miles per hour then the acceleration could have been calculated as follows.

$$\text{acceleration} = \frac{\text{change in speed}}{\text{time taken for change}}$$

$$= \frac{(50 - 30) \text{ miles per hour}}{3 \text{ seconds}}$$

$$= 6 \cdot 6 \text{ miles per hour per second}$$

Speed-time graphs

8. An object's motion can be described by a speed-time graph. Speed-time graphs representing constant speed and acceleration, i.e. speeding up or slowing down, are given below.

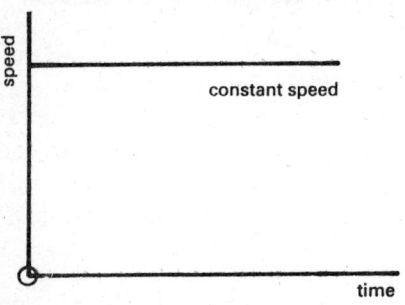

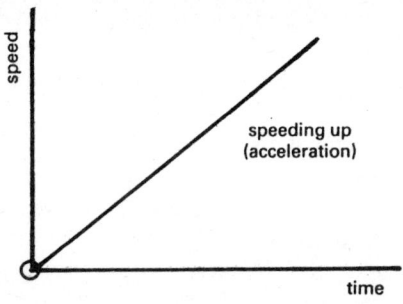

88

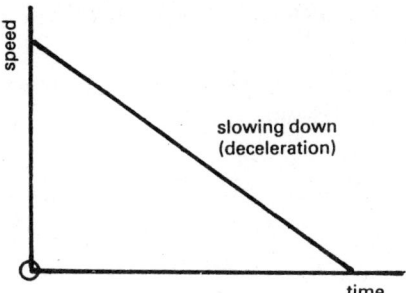

Make sure that you can draw these graphs for each type of motion.

9. You should also be able to interpret a speed-time graph and describe the type of motion which is taking place.

An example of the kind of graph which you might be expected to interpret is as follows.

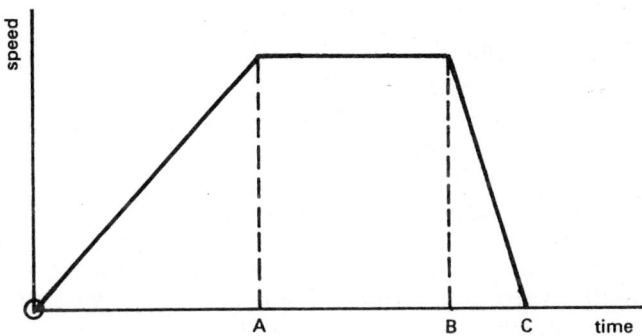

The motion of a car is represented by the speed-time graph shown above. Describe the motion of the car during the periods OA, AB and BC.

During OA the car has an acceleration and is speeding up. During AB the car has a constant speed. During BC the car is decelerating and is slowing down.

10. Calculate the value of a constant acceleration from information provided on a speed-time graph. A constant acceleration is one where the object's speed changes by the same amount every second.

89

An example of the kind of calculating that is expected of you is as follows.

Calculate the value of the acceleration which is described by the following speed-time graph.

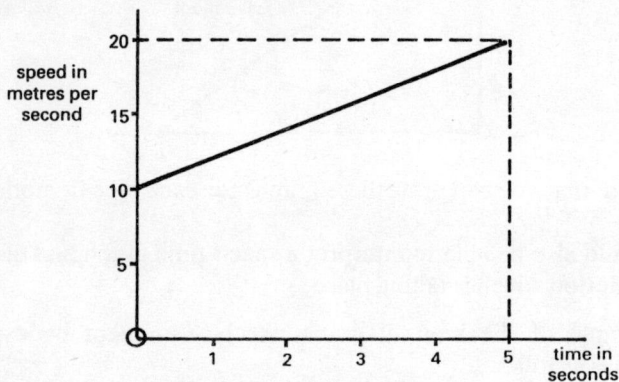

change in speed = (20 − 10) metres per second

time taken for change = 5 seconds

$$\text{acceleration} = \frac{\text{change in speed}}{\text{time taken for change}}$$
$$= \frac{10 \text{ metres per second}}{5 \text{ seconds}}$$
$$= 2 \text{ metres per second per second}$$

11. *Calculate the acceleration of an object and the distance travelled by it from speed-time graphs of its motion. The motion can involve more than one constant acceleration.*

   In order to carry out the calculation, you will have to remember that distance travelled is represented by the area under the speed-time graph.

   An example of the kind of calculating that might be expected of you is as follows.

   Use the information provided on the speed-time graph on the following page to calculate:

   (i) the acceleration during the period 3 s to 6 s;

   (ii) the distance travelled during the period 0 to 6 s.

90

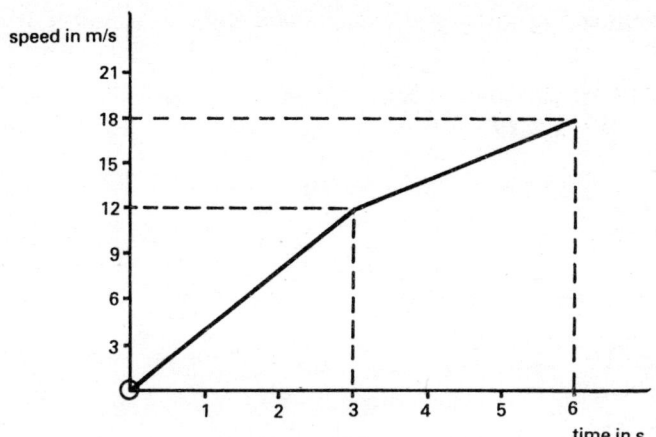

(i) $acceleration = \dfrac{change\ in\ speed}{time\ taken\ for\ change}$

$= \dfrac{18 - 12}{3}$

$= \dfrac{6}{3}$

$= 2\ m/s^2$

(ii) *distance travelled = area under graph*

= area under 0 to 3 s section + area under 3 to 6 s section

Area under 0 to 3 s section $= \dfrac{1}{2} \times 3 \times 12 = 18\ m$

Area under 3 to 6 s section $= (3 \times 12) + \left(\dfrac{1}{2} \times 3 \times 6\right)$

$= 36 + 9 = 45\ m$

Distance travelled in 0 to 6 s $= 18 + 45$

$= 63\ m$

12. *At Credit Level, it is expected that you should be able to use the relationship* $a = \dfrac{v - u}{t}$ *in carrying out calculations involving a constant acceleration.*

This relationship is derived from the definition of acceleration. The term 'a' represents the acceleration, 'v' is the final speed, 'u' the initial speed and 't' the time taken for the speed to change.

91

An example of the kind of calculating that might be expected of you is as follows.

An object has a uniform acceleration. The object's speed changes from 25 m/s to 10 m/s in a time of 5 s. What is the acceleration of the object?

$u = 25 \, m/s$

$v = 10 \, m/s$

$t = 5 \, s$

$a = \dfrac{v - u}{t}$

$a = \dfrac{10 - 25}{5}$

$= \dfrac{-15}{5}$

$= -3 \, m/s^2$

At Credit Level, you should be able to recognise what is meant by the negative sign in the value which the relationship gives for the acceleration. The negative sign indicates that the speed is decreasing with time, i.e. the object is slowing down or decelerating.

SECTION 2:   FORCES

Effects of force

1. When a force is applied to an object, it can produce a number of effects. The force can change the shape of the object. It can also change the speed and the direction of motion of the object.

Measuring force

2. The newton balance uses the change in shape of a spring to give a measure of the size of a force in newtons.

    The extension of the spring is directly proportional to the size of the force which is applied to the spring. This is a mathematical way of saying that when the force applied to the spring is doubled then so does the stretch of the spring. Three times the force gives three times the stretch and so on. The stretch of the spring is read against a scale of force marked in newtons on the balance.

3. Weight is a force and is measured in newtons. Weight is a pulling force. The weight of an object (on Earth) is the pull that the Earth has for the object.

At the surface of the Earth, the pull of the Earth on a mass of 1 kilogram is approximately 10 newtons. The Earth pulls with a force of approximately 20 newtons on a mass of 2 kilograms as so on.

You are expected to be able to use this value of 10 newtons per kilogram to calculate the weight of an object.

An example of the kind of calculating that might be expected of you is as follows.

A crate has a mass of 30 kilograms. What is the weight of the crate?

the pull of the Earth on 1 kilogram = 10 newtons
the pull of the Earth on 30 kilograms is 30 × 10 = 300 newtons
the weight of the crate = 300 newtons

4. *The pull of the Earth on a mass of 1 kilogram is referred to as the Earth's gravitational field strength. Weight per unit mass is gravitational field strength.*

$$\frac{weight}{mass} = gravitational\ field\ strength$$

$$\frac{w}{m} = g$$

The weight of an object is therefore given by the following relationship

$$w = mg$$

Close to the surface of the Earth the value of g is approximately 10 N/kg.

5. *Mass and weight are different quantities. The mass of an object can be thought of as a measure of the amount of matter in the object. Mass is measured in kilograms. Weight is a force. It is measured in newtons and is the gravitational pull on an object.*

Friction and movement

6.   Friction is a force. It is a force which can oppose the motion of an object.

7.   Sometimes it is desirable to increase friction so that it will provide a large force. For example, a friction force on the rim of a bicycle wheel enables the bicycle to be slowed down and brought to a stop. The friction force is provided by a brake pad rubbing on the rim of the wheel. The design of the brake pad is such that it gives a friction force large enough to slow down quickly the motion of the wheel.

On other occasions, it is desirable to decrease the size of the friction force. In downhill ski racing, for example, the skis are waxed to reduce the friction force from the snow on the skis. The force opposing the motion of the skier is reduced and this enables a quicker descent.

Newton's First Law

8.   Forces of the same size but acting in opposite directions on a body are called balanced forces.

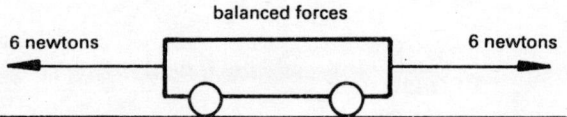

Balanced forces acting on a body produce the same type of motion as no forces acting on the body.

9.   If a body is at rest and the forces acting on it are balanced, the body will remain at rest. However, if a body is moving and the forces acting on it are balanced, the body will keep moving at a constant speed. This statement about motion under balanced forces was made by Isaac Newton and is referred to as Newton's First Law of Motion.

10.   *At Credit Level, you are expected to be able to explain the movement of objects in terms of Newton's First Law.*

For example, a vehicle is supported on an air track by a cushion of air. The vehicle moves backwards and forwards along the track at a constant speed.

The motion of the vehicle can be explained in terms of Newton's First Law. The vertical forces acting on the vehicle are balanced.

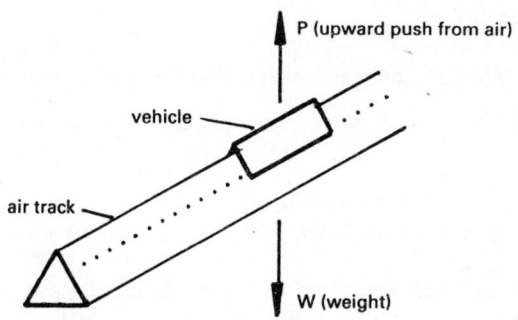

The upwards push from the air balances the downward pull of the weight of the vehicle. There are (almost) no forces acting horizontally because of the very low friction provided by the track. The motion of the vehicle therefore complies with Newton's First Law — it moves backwards and forwards along the track with a constant speed under the action of balanced forces.

There are many other instances where the motion can be interpreted in terms of the First Law. For example, sky divers can fall through the air at a constant speed. This motion can be explained in terms of Newton's First Law as follows.

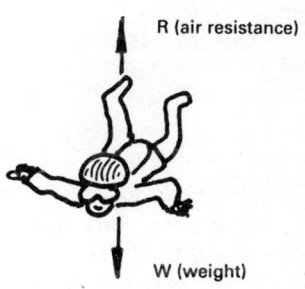

The forces acting on the sky diver must be balanced forces.

The downward pull by the force of gravity is balanced by the upwards resistive force from the air.

Newton's Second Law

11. Newton's Second Law is concerned with unbalanced forces and the effect these have on motion. Newton's Second Law gives a relationship between the unbalanced force, the mass of the object to which the force is applied and the acceleration which the force produces.

95

The larger the unbalanced force acting on the object, the bigger its acceleration.

The bigger the mass of the object, the smaller its acceleration (for a given unbalanced force).

12. Newton's Second Law can be stated mathematically as follows.

$$\text{unbalanced force} = \text{mass} \times \text{acceleration}$$
$$F = ma$$

F is measured in newtons, m is measured in kilograms and the acceleration is measured in metres per second per second.

13. Carry out calculations using Newton's Second Law. At General Level, the calculations will involve finding the value for F, m or a, given any two of these quantities.

An example of the kind of calculating that might be expected of you is as follows.

A vehicle has a mass of 500 kilograms. An unbalanced force of 1500 newtons acts on the vehicle. What acceleration is produced by the force?

$$F = ma$$
$$1500 = 500 \times a$$
$$a = \frac{1500}{500}$$
$$= 3 \text{ metres per second per second.}$$

14 *At Credit Level, in carrying out calculations involving Newton's Second Law, you may first of all have to calculate the unbalanced force. An example of the type of Credit Level calculation which you might have to perform is as follows.*

Three forces are applied to an object of mass 5 kg as shown in the diagram below.

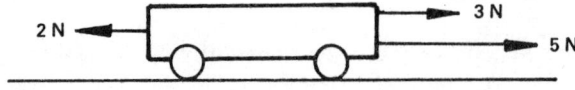

What is the acceleration of the object?

unbalanced force acting on the object $= 5 + 3 - 2$
$$= 6\,N$$

$F = ma$

$a = \dfrac{F}{m}$

$\quad = \dfrac{6}{5}$

$\quad = 1 \cdot 2\,m/s^2$

acceleration produced by forces $= 1 \cdot 2\,m/s^2$

Seat belts and Newton's Laws

15. An explanation in terms of Newton's Laws as to why seat belts are required in cars is as follows.

   When a car is travelling at a constant speed, the forces on the car, by Newton's First Law, are balanced. The driver of the car is also travelling at a constant speed. The forces acting on the driver are also balanced.

   If another force is applied to the car, either through the application of the brakes or by the impact of a collision, then, by Newton's Second Law, the car will slow down, i.e. decelerate. It is important that the driver of the car, and its passengers, slow down at the same rate as the car. If this is not the case, they will continue to travel forward and perhaps collide with the windscreen of the car and each other. Serious injury could result.

   A large force is required to decelerate the occupants of the car and slow them down at the same rate as the car. The force is applied through the wearing of seat belts. When the car is decelerating, the seat belts apply forces to the driver and the passengers and bring them to rest at the same time as the car, thereby reducing the risk of injury.

SECTION 3:   MOVEMENT MEANS ENERGY

Kinetic energy and gravitational potential energy

1. You are expected to be able to describe motion using the terms 'kinetic energy' and 'gravitational potential energy'.

   For example, suppose a bicycle is accelerated by its rider. Energy is transferred to the bicycle as it speeds up. The bicycle gains energy.

The energy which is associated with the movement is called kinetic energy.

When the bicycle travels at a constant speed, its kinetic energy does not change. When the bicycle is braked and slowed down, energy is transferred. Its kinetic energy becomes less and heat is produced.

Suppose the bicycle is now allowed to free-wheel up a slope. As the bicycle travels up the slope, it slows down. Energy is transferred. The kinetic energy of the bicycle becomes less. It loses kinetic energy and gains what is called gravitational potential energy. The gravitational potential energy of the bicycle depends on its position on the slope. The higher up the slope the greater the gravitational potential energy of the bicycle.

If the bicycle is now allowed to free-wheel back down the slope, its speed will increase. Energy is transferred to the bicycle. There is now a loss of gravitational potential energy and a gain in kinetic energy.

2. The kinetic energy of an object depends on the mass and the speed of the object. The greater the speed of the object, the greater the kinetic energy associated with it. The more mass the moving object has, the greater its kinetic energy.

3. *Kinetic energy is given by the following relationship.*

$$kinetic\ energy = \frac{1}{2} \times mass \times speed^2$$

$$E_k = \frac{1}{2}mv^2$$

Kinetic energy is measured in joules, mass is measured in kilograms and speed is measured in metres/second.

4. *Carry out calculations involving the relationship between kinetic energy, mass and speed.*

An example of the kind of calculating that might be expected of you is as follows.

A car has mass of 1500 kg. It has a kinetic energy of 300 000 J. What is the speed of the car?

$$E_k = \frac{1}{2}mv^2$$
$$v^2 = 2 \times \frac{300\,000}{1500}$$
$$= 400$$
$$v = 20\,m/s$$
speed of car = 20 m/s

Work and energy

5. When a force is applied to an object and the object is then moved a certain distance, work is done by the force.

    The work done by the force leads to a transfer of energy. The transfer of energy could result in an increase in the kinetic energy of the object. Alternatively, the transfer of energy could result in a decrease in kinetic energy of the object and the production of heat.

    The work done by the force could also lead to an increase in the gravitational potential energy of the object.

6. The work done by a force is measured by the product of the force, measured in newtons, and the distance, measured in metres, over which the force is moved.

    $$\text{Work done} = \text{force} \times \text{distance}$$
    $$W = Fd$$

    Work done is measured in joules.

7. Carry out calculations involving the relationship between work done, force and distance.

    An example of the kind of calculating that might be expected of you is as follows.

    > A garage mechanic pushes a car with a force of 150 newtons. The car is pushed over a distance of 5 metres. How much work is done by the mechanic?

    $W = Fd$
    $\quad = 150 \times 5$
    $\quad = 750\,\text{joules}$

    Work done by mechanic = 750 joules

99

8. Power is work done per second or energy transferred per second. Power is given by the following relationship.

$$\text{Power} = \frac{\text{work done}}{\text{time}} = \frac{\text{energy transferred}}{\text{time}}$$

$$P = \frac{W}{t}$$

Power is measured in watts. A power of 1 watt indicates that 1 joule of work is done every second.

9. Carry out calculations involving the relationship between power, work done and time.

An example of the kind of calculating that might be expected of you is as follows.

> A worker does 1400 joules of work in raising a load. The worker takes 5 seconds to raise the load. What is the power of the worker?

work done = 1400 joules

$$\text{power of worker} = \frac{W}{t} = \frac{1400}{5}$$

$$= 280 \text{ watts}$$

10. When an object is lifted so that its position is raised, we say that 'work has been done against gravity'. The lifting of the object causes a gain in the gravitational potential energy of the object. The gain in the object's gravitational potential energy is equal to the work which has been done against gravity.

When an object is lowered, we say 'work has been done by gravity'. In this case, there is a decrease in the gravitational potential energy of the object.

The gravitational potential energy, E_p, of an object at a height, h, is given by the following relationship.

$$E_p = mgh$$

   m is the mass of the object in kilograms
   g is the pull of the Earth on a mass of 1 kilogram near the surface of the Earth (10 newtons per kilogram)
   h is measured in metres

Gravitational potential energy is measured in joules.

100

Conservation of energy

11. *An important law of physics states that energy is conserved, i.e. energy cannot be created or destroyed. This means that at any time there is always the same amount of energy in existence. Energy can be transferred but the total amount of energy present does not vary.*

12. *Carry out calculations involving the law of conservation of energy.*

   An example of the kind of calculating that might be expected of you is as follows.

   > *A trolley of mass 2 kg is given a speed of 4 m/s at the bottom of a ramp. The trolley then travels up the ramp. At a vertical height of 0·5 m up the ramp, the trolley's speed is 1·5 m/s.*
   >
   > *(a) What is the kinetic energy of the trolley at the bottom of the ramp?*
   >
   > *(b) What is the gravitational potential energy and kinetic energy associated with the trolley when it is at a vertical height of 0·5 m?*
   >
   > *(c) What is the work done against friction in moving the trolley to the vertical height of 0·5 m?*

   (a) kinetic energy $= \frac{1}{2}mv^2$

   $$= \frac{1}{2} \times 2 \times 4 \times 4$$
   $$= 16\,J$$

   (b) gravitational potential energy at 0·5 metres $= mgh$
   $$= 2 \times 10 \times 0\cdot5$$
   $$- 10\,J$$

   kinetic energy at 0·5 metres $= \frac{1}{2}mv^2$

   $$= \frac{1}{2} \times 2 \times 1\cdot5 \times 1\cdot5$$
   $$= 2\cdot25\,J$$

(c) *total energy associated with the trolley = 16 J*

kinetic energy and gravitational potential energy at 0·5 m = 10 + 2·25
= 12·25 J

energy transferred = 16 − 12·25
= 3·75 J

work done against friction = 3·75 J

UNIT 6 — ENERGY MATTERS

The table below lists the sections and content of the Unit on Energy Matters.

Section	Content
1. Supply and demand	Main sources of energy
	Non-renewable sources
	Renewable sources
	Calculating supply and demand
2. Generation of electricity	Power stations
	Pumped hydro-electric scheme
	Nuclear power
3. Source to consumer	Induced voltage
	Alternating current generator
	Transformers
	National grid
4. Heat in the home	Heat and temperature
	Heat losses in the house by conduction, convection and radiation
	Specific heat capacity
	Change of state
	Latent heat
	Specific latent heat of fusion and vaporisation

The paragraphs in italics describe the additional knowledge which is needed for the Credit Level examination.

SECTION 1:   SUPPLY AND DEMAND

Main sources of energy

1. Fossil fuels are at present our main sources of energy. These fuels occur naturally in the Earth and have been formed over a period of millions of years from decomposed prehistoric plants and animals. Examples of fossil fuels are coal, oil, natural gas and peat.

Non-renewable sources

2. The reserves of fossil fuels are finite. This means that the reserves are limited and there will be a day when these are all used up. Fossil fuels are, therefore, described as non-renewable sources.

    Another example of a non-renewable source is uranium. Uranium is the fuel which is used in nuclear reactors.

Renewable sources

3. Other sources of energy such as the sun, tides, wind, waves and hydro-power are classified as renewable sources. These sources will last as long as we have sun, sea, wind, waves and water!

4. *At Credit Level, it is expected that you can describe the advantages and disadvantages of at least three renewable sources. You might wish to consider sun, wind, waves and water.*

    The advantage of all these sources is that by using them we can conserve our limited stocks of fossil fuels. In addition, the renewable sources are 'clean'. This means that they can all be used to produce electricity directly without creating the pollutants which cause acid rain, as is the case with fossil fuels. In addition, the use of these sources to produce electricity does not involve the production of carbon dioxide which causes the 'greenhouse effect' in our atmosphere.

The sources, however, do have their disadvantages. For example, the sun does not always shine when we want it to, especially in the UK! The solar panels which would use the heat from the sun to produce electricity do not work well enough in dull conditions.

Wind and waves are also not always available when you need them. Many wind and water machines would be needed to cope with the current demand for energy. There is a worry too, that the siting of these machines could spoil our environment and the scenic beauty of our landscapes and coastlines.

Calculating supply and demand

5. Carry out calculations relating to energy supply and demand. An example of the kind of calculating that might be expected of you is as follows.

    Nuclear power stations and wind generators can be used to meet the demand for electricity. The table below shows the electrical power supplied by a wind generator and a nuclear power station.

	Power output in millions of watts (megawatts)
Wind generator	3
Nuclear power station	1200

    How many wind generators would have to be built to supply the same power as the nuclear power station?

    $$\text{number of wind generators} = \frac{1200}{3}$$
    $$= 400$$

Conserving energy

6. 'Conserving energy' means being efficient in the way we use our sources of energy. You are expected to be able to explain one means of conserving energy related to the use of energy in industry, the home and in transport. Some examples are as follows.

In industry, it is important that large areas of work space are properly illuminated. In many factories, new technology fluorescent tubes are being fitted. These new fittings produce the equivalent lighting of existing fittings but for much less power. Considerable energy savings are thereby made.

Loft insulation, cavity wall insulation and double glazing reduce the rate at which heat escapes from the home. Less heat has to be produced by the heating system to keep the temperature of the air in the home at a comfortable level. Fuel consumption is therefore reduced.

In transport, engines are designed with electronic ignition and management systems. These systems make the engines more efficient in terms of miles per gallon. Attention is also given to the aerodynamic design of car body shapes. A streamlined body shape reduces the resistance force due to the air. Less work has to be done against the resistance forces. Streamlined cars are therefore generally more economical with fuel.

SECTION 2:   GENERATION OF ELECTRICITY

Power stations

1. Make sure that you can identify, from diagrams, how energy is transferred by a thermal power station, a hydro-electric power station and a nuclear power station.

   Thermal and nuclear stations work in more or less the same way. A diagram showing the operation of these power stations is given below.

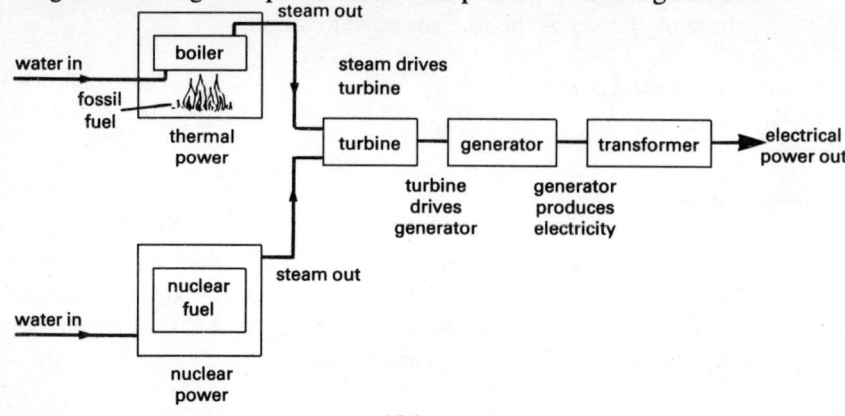

In these stations, the source of the energy is the fuel. The thermal stations burn fossil fuel to produce heat. In the nuclear station, uranium fuel undergoes a process called nuclear fission and, in so doing, releases large amounts of heat.

The heat from the fossil or uranium fuel is used to heat water to produce steam. The steam drives a turbine which, in turn, drives a generator which produces electricity. Electricity is the means by which the energy from the fuel source is transferred to the consumer.

In the hydro-electric power station, the source of the energy is the gravitational potential energy of a large mass of water stored in a high reservoir. A diagram showing the operation of a hydro-electric power station is shown below.

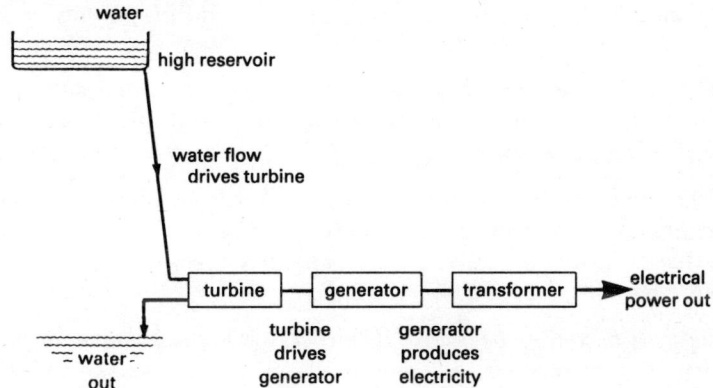

The water flows down from the reservoir through pipes and drives a turbine which, in turn, drives a generator which produces electricity. The electricity then transfers energy to the consumer.

2. Carry out calculations on energy transferred by power stations. An example of the kind of calculating that might be expected of you is as follows.

    The dam of a hydro-electric power station is 50 metres above the turbine.

    What mass of water must flow from the dam in order to deliver 1 000 000 joules of energy to the turbine?

loss of gravitational potential energy = mgh

mgh = 1 000 000

$$m = \frac{1\,000\,000}{(10 \times 50)}$$

= 2000 kilograms

A mass of 2000 kilograms would need to flow from the dam to the turbine.

3. *The energy transferred to consumers by a power station is always less than the energy which is delivered by the fuel. In a typical power station, perhaps only 35% of the energy which is delivered by the fuel reaches the consumers. This is because energy is being transferred as heat to the surroundings at various stages of the power producing process.*

4. *We talk about the world running out of energy. Yet in physics we say that energy is conserved. These two statements seem to be at odds with each other. How can we be running out of energy and yet still have energy?*

    The point is that our 'conserved energy' is becoming less useful. We are not running out of energy, we are running out of 'usefulness'. Each time an appliance such as a toaster, a TV or a lamp is operated, the energy which is transferred becomes of a poorer quality.

    Energy is becoming begraded. The energy is not as suitable for producing electricity, for example, as it once was when it was stored as fuel. Energy is becoming less useful.

5. *The efficiency of a power station is defined as energy transferred at its output divided by the energy it obtains from its fuel source.*

    $$efficiency = \frac{energy\ transferred\ at\ output}{energy\ delivered\ at\ input}$$

    The energy transferred from the power station to the consumer is always less than the energy obtained from its fuel source. The efficiency of power stations is therefore always less than 100%.

6. *You should be able to carry out calculations on the efficiency of power stations.*

An example of the kind of calculating that is expected of you is as follows.

A power station has an efficiency of 40%. 80 MJ of energy is transferred to the consumers. How much energy is obtained from its fuel source?

$$efficiency = \frac{energy\ transferred\ at\ output}{energy\ delivered\ at\ input}$$

$$\frac{40}{100} = \frac{80}{energy\ delivered\ at\ input}$$

$$energy\ delivered\ at\ input = \frac{80}{0\cdot4} = 200\ MJ$$

energy obtained from fuel source = 200 MJ

Pumped hydro-electric scheme

7. The demand for electricity is not steady. Late on at night, the demand is usually low. During this period, water can be pumped back up to the reservoir of a hydro-electric power station to increase its store of gravitational potential energy. Water can then be released from the reservoir during periods when the demand for electricity is high.

The advantage of a pumped hydro-electric scheme is that it is an economical and efficient way of producing electricity. When demand is low, a pumped hydro-electric scheme makes use of the spare capacity of other power stations to renew its energy store. In addition, it is able to top up its energy store to some extent by using natural sources such as rainwater.

Nuclear power

8. *In a nuclear power station, the energy source is uranium. If a neutron hits the nucleus of an atom of uranium, the nucleus can split. The splitting of the nucleus is called nuclear fission. The splitting of a nucleus produces heat.*

The amount of heat produced by a single fission is small. However, during one fission more neutrons are produced. These neutrons produce more fissions, which produce more heat and more neutrons. Further fissions then take place and so the process goes on in a kind of chain as shown in the diagram below.

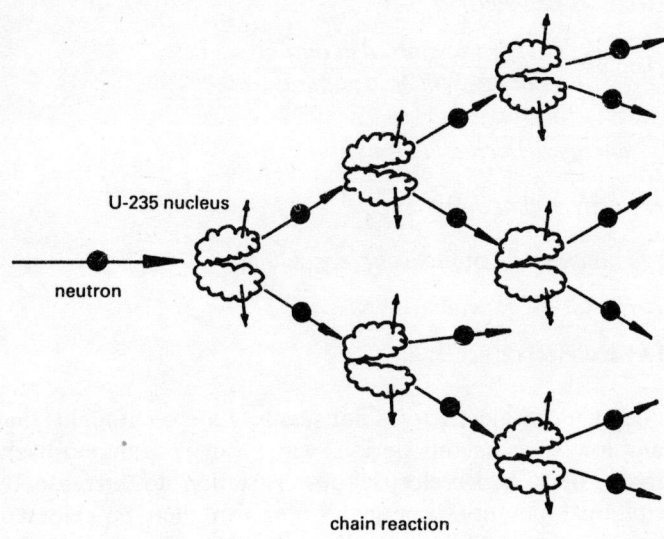

chain reaction

This process of producing a large amount of heat from uranium is called a chain reaction.

9. The splitting of the uranium nucleii in the reactor of a nuclear power station leads to the production of nucleii which are highly radioactive. These fragments of the uranium nucleus are the waste products of the nuclear power station. The fragments can be thought of as a kind of 'hot ash'. The fragments of 'ash' stay radioactive or 'hot' for a long period of time.

10. *Nuclear power stations produce more energy per kilogram of fuel than thermal power stations. At Credit Level, you are expected to be able to compare the energy output from equal masses of uranium and coal.*

    An example of the kind of comparison you might be expected to make is as follows.

The table below gives information on the energy extracted from 1 kg of coal and 1 kg of uranium fuel.

Fuel	Energy output
Coal	28 megajoules
Uranium	5·6 terajoules

How many kilograms of coal are needed to give the same energy output as a kilogram of uranium?

$$mass\ of\ coal\ required = \frac{5 \cdot 6 \times 10^{12}}{28 \times 10^{6}}$$
$$= 200\ 000\ kg$$
$$= 200\ tonnes$$

SECTION 3: SOURCE TO CONSUMER

Induced voltage

1. When a conductor is moved so that it cuts through a magnetic field, a voltage is induced in the conductor. A voltage is also induced when the conductor is held stationary and the magnetic field is moved. Relative motion between conductor and magnetic field causes an induced voltage.

Alternating current generator

2. You should be able to identify in a diagram the main parts of an alternating current generator. A simple diagram is given below.

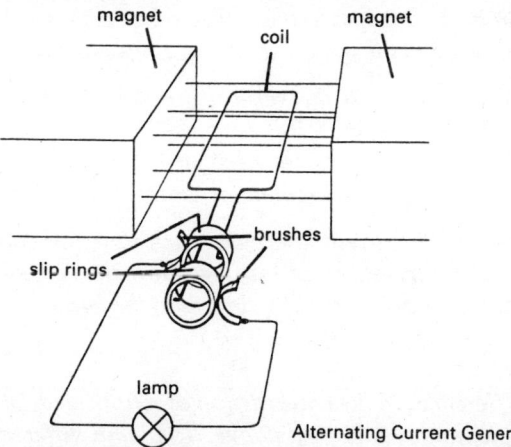

Alternating Current Generator

Make sure that you can identify the coil, magnet, slip rings and brushes.

111

3. *The operation of the generator shown in paragraph 2 on the previous page can be explained as follows.*

    Suppose the coil rotates clockwise as shown in the diagram below.

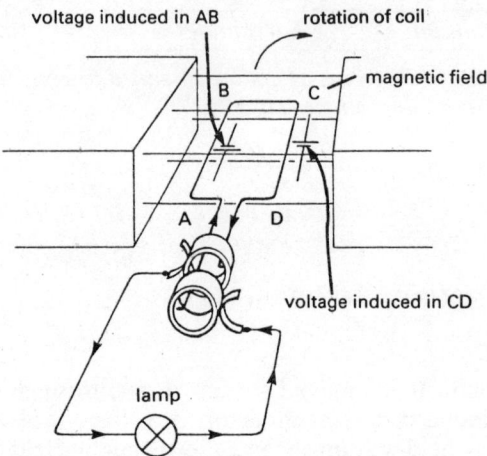

The right hand side of the coil moves downwards and the left hand side of the coil moves upwards, cutting through the magnetic field. A voltage is induced in each side of the coil.

These induced voltages act just like two small batteries connected + to – in series. The induced voltages in the coil cause a current to be produced. The current is delivered to the lamp via the slip rings and the brushes.

When the coil rotates past the vertical position, the direction of voltages induced in each side of the coil is reversed. The induced voltages now act as though the two small batteries were turned the other way around. As a result, the direction of the current in the lamp is also reversed.

The direction of the current alternates each time the coil rotates through 180 degrees. The slip rings and brushes allow the coil to rotate freely and enable it to produce an alternating current in the lamp.

4. *There are differences in the construction of a full-sized, practical generator and the simple model described above. The main difference is that instead of having a stationary permanent magnet and a moving coil, the full-sized*

generator has a rotating electromagnet, called a rotor, and a stationary coil, called a stator.

The size of the voltage which is induced in the stator coils depends on the number of turns in these coils. It also depends on the strength of the magnetic field provided by the electromagnet and the speed of rotation of the rotor.

Transformers

5. Transformers are devices which are used to transform or change the size of one alternating voltage to another. The transformer consists of an iron core on which are wound two coils as shown in the diagram below.

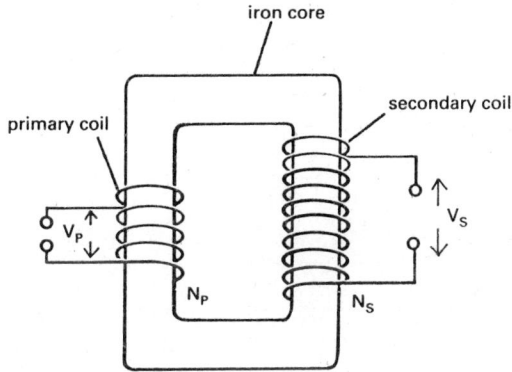

One coil is called the primary coil and the other is called the secondary coil.

In a transformer, the voltage V_p across the primary coil and the voltage V_s across the secondary coil are related to the number of turns N_p in the primary and the number of turns N_s in the secondary coil. The relationship is as follows.

$$\frac{V_s}{V_p} = \frac{N_s}{N_p}$$

6. Carry out calculations using the following relationship.

$$\frac{V_s}{V_p} = \frac{N_s}{N_p}$$

An example of the kind of calculating that might be expected of you is as follows.

> The primary coil of a transformer has 50 turns. A 5 volt alternating voltage is applied to the primary coil. The voltage across the secondary coil is 20 volts. How many turns are on the secondary coil?

$$\frac{V_s}{V_p} = \frac{20}{5} = \frac{4}{1} = \frac{N_s}{N_p}$$

$$N_s = 4 \times 50 = 200$$

number of turns on secondary coil = 200

7. *The efficiency of a transformer is defined as follows.*

$$efficiency = \frac{power\ obtained\ from\ secondary}{power\ delivered\ to\ primary}$$

$$= \frac{V_s \times I_s}{V_p \times I_p}$$

V_p and V_s are the primary and secondary voltages. I_p is the current in the primary coil and I_s is the current in the secondary coil.

If a transformer is 100% efficient, then the power which is delivered to the primary coil is equal to the power which is obtained from the secondary coil.

8. *In practice, transformers do not transfer the same power from the secondary coil as is delivered to the primary coil. There are always some power losses. Power losses can be accounted for as follows.*

The coils have some resistance and so heat is produced in the coils. The changing magnetic field around the coils induces small currents in the core. These currents produce heat.

In addition, some energy is transferred as heat due to the core being continually magnetised and demagnetised.

Thus, the energy which is transferred by the secondary coil is always less than that which is supplied to the primary coil. In practice, though, the

114

losses are not too serious. Most transformers are nearly 100% efficient.

9. *Carry out calculations on transformers. The calculations could involve you in using primary and secondary voltages and currents, turns ratio and efficiency.*

   An example of the kind of calculating that might be expected of you is as follows.

   A 24 W lamp is connected across the secondary coil of a transformer. The lamp operates at its normal brightness. The voltage supplied to the primary coil is 2 V. The transformer is 95% efficient. Calculate the current in the primary coil.

   $$efficiency = \frac{power\ obtained\ from\ secondary}{power\ delivered\ to\ primary}$$

   $$= \frac{96}{100} = 0 \cdot 96$$

   $$power\ delivered\ to\ primary = \frac{power\ obtained\ from\ secondary}{0 \cdot 96} = \frac{24}{0 \cdot 96}$$

   $$= 25\ W$$

   $$V_p \times I_p = 25$$
   $$2 \times I_p = 25$$
   $$I_p = 12 \cdot 5\ A$$

   current in the primary coil $= 12 \cdot 5\ A$

National Grid

10. Electricity is transmitted throughout the country by means of a network or grid of transmission lines. Pylons carry the transmission lines to all parts of the country. The network of pylons and transmission lines is called the National Grid.

    Power stations are linked to the National Grid by large transformers. These transformers, called step-up transformers, enable electrical power to be supplied to the grid at high voltage. Transformers are also used to enable power to be drawn from the grid and delivered to the factories, hospitals and homes. These transformers are called step-down transformers. They step down the high voltage on the cables of the transmission line to a voltage which is suitable for factory machinery and the electrical appliances in the home.

A simple diagram of the grid system is given below.

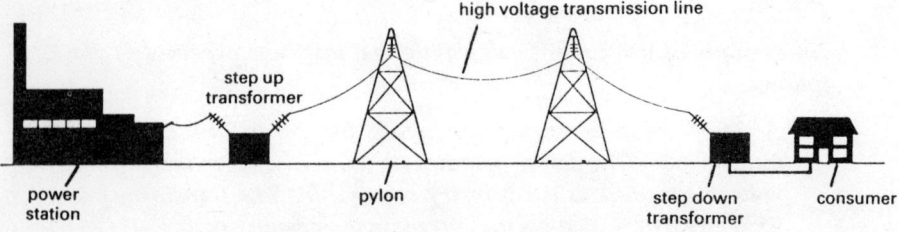

11. The transformers which link the power stations with the National Grid supply high voltages to the electricity transmission cables. High voltages are used in order to reduce power losses in the transmission cables. Heat is produced in the cables during the transmission of electricity. Much more heat would be produced if lower voltages were used for transmission. High voltages cut down on the production of heat in the cables.

12. *At Credit Level, you are expected to carry out calculations relating to power loss in electrical transmission cables.*

   An example of the kind of calculating that might be expected of you is as follows.

   100 MW of power is delivered by a transformer to an electrical transmission line. The transformer supplies a voltage of 400 000 V to the line. The resistance of the cable in the line is 4 Ω.

   Calculate the power losses in the cable.

   power delivered to cable $= V \times I$
   $$100\,000\,000 = 400\,000 \times I$$
   $$I = 250\,A$$
   power produced by cable $= I^2R$
   $$= 250 \times 250 \times 4$$
   $$= 250\,000\,W$$
   power losses in the cable $= 250\,kW$

116

SECTION 4:   HEAT IN THE HOME

Heat and temperature

1. Make sure that you able to use correctly the terms temperature, Celsius and heat.

    Temperature is a measure of the hotness or coldness of something. Temperature can be measured using the Celsius scale.

    Heat is something which flows from a hot to a cold body. Heat is associated with energy. Heat is measured in joules.

Heat losses in the home by conduction, convection and radiation

2. Heat can be moved from place to place by three methods — conduction, convection and radiation. You are expected to describe ways of reducing the heat that is lost from the home by conduction, convection and radiation.

    For example, a mineral wool type of material placed in the loft and below the floor boards can reduce heat losses by conduction. The fibres of the material trap air, which is a poor conductor of heat.

    Double glazing is another method of using air to cut down on heat losses by conduction. The layer of air trapped between the double panes of glass acts as a heat insulator.

    The heat lost every second due to conduction depends on the inside and outside air temperatures. The bigger the difference between these two temperatures, the greater the heat lost every second from the home. Heat losses in the home will therefore be greatest in winter.

    Heat losses by convection in the cavity in the wall of the home can be reduced by filling the cavity with foam or mineral wool. The foam and the wool do not allow the air to move and thereby prevent convection currents being set up in the cavity.

    Radiation losses can be reduced through the use of plasterboard sheets which are backed with metal foil. The metal foil reflects heat back towards the inside of the room and slows down the rate at which heat is lost by radiation. Metal foil fixed to the wall behind radiators has a similar effect.

Specific heat capacity

3. Different amounts of heat are needed to raise the temperature of the same mass of different substances by 1 celsius degree.

    The specific heat capacity of a substance is the heat needed to raise the temperature of 1 kilogram of the substance by 1 celsius degree. Specific heat capacity is measured in joules per kilogram per celsius degree.

4. The heat E_h which has to be supplied to a material of mass m kilograms and specific heat capacity c in order to raise its temperature by ΔT celsius degrees is given by the following relationship.

    $$E_h = cm\Delta T$$

5. Carry out calculations using the relationship $E_h = cm\Delta T$.

    An example of the kind of calculating that might be expected of you is as follows.

    A heater supplies 13 500 joules of energy to a metal block. The specific heat capacity of the metal is 450 joules per kilogram per celsius degree. The temperature of the block rises from 15 degrees celsius to 75 degrees celsius.

    What is the mass of the copper block?

    $E_h = cm\Delta T$

    $m = \dfrac{E_h}{c\Delta T}$

    $= \dfrac{13\,500}{450 \times 60}$

    $= 0 \cdot 5$

    mass of block $= 0 \cdot 5$ kilogram

6. *At Credit Level, you are expected to be able to do calculations on heating by making use of the Law of Conservation of Energy.*

    An example of the kind of calculating that might be expected of you is as follows.

The temperature of a lump of metal of mass 0·5 kg is raised from 20 °C to 40 °C in 110 s by a heater of power 50 W. What is the specific heat capacity of this metal?

energy transferred by heater = heat energy gained by metal

$$power \times time = cm\Delta T$$
$$50 \times 110 = c \times 0·5 \times 20$$
$$c = \frac{50 \times 110}{0·5 \times 20}$$
$$= 550 \, J/kg \, °C$$

specific heat capacity of metal = 550 J/kg °C

Change of state

7. Supplying heat to a substance or removing heat from it may cause the substance to change its state. Change of state means changing from a solid to a liquid (fusion) or changing from liquid to solid (freezing). Change of state also includes a liquid changing to a vapour (vaporisation) or a vapour changing to a liquid (condensation).

8. When a substancce is changing its state, the temperature of the substance does not change. For example, ice at 0 °C on changing state becomes water at 0 °C.

Latent heat

9. The heat which is needed to change a solid at its melting point into a liquid is called the latent heat of fusion of the solid.

   A change of state can also involve a liquid at its boiling point being changed to a vapour. The heat needed to do this is called the latent heat of vaporisation of the liquid.

10. When a change of state is such that a liquid changes back to a solid, or a vapour changes back to a liquid, heat is given out.

    Energy is released or gained by a substance when it changes state.

11. A refrigerator is an example of a household appliance which makes use of latent heat and change of state. A liquid, called Freon, is used in the cooling system of the refrigerator. Heat is taken from the interior of the fridge and used to make the Freon change from a liquid to a vapour. The removal of heat from the interior of the fridge causes the temperature of the air in the fridge to be lowered. The contents of the fridge are therefore kept cool.

Specific latent heat of fusion and vaporisation

12. *The heat which is needed to change the state of 1 kilogram of a solid at its melting point into liquid is called the specific latent heat of fusion of the liquid. Specific latent heat of fusion is measured in joules per kilogram.*

13. *The heat E_h in joules which is needed to change the state of a solid of mass m kg at its melting point into a liquid is given by the following relationship.*

$$E_h = mL_f$$

L_f is the specific latent heat of fusion of the solid.

The heat which is needed to change 1 kilogram of a liquid at its boiling point into vapour is called the specific latent heat of vaporisation of the liquid. Specific latent heat of vaporisation is measured in joules per kilogram.

14. *The heat E_h in joules which is needed to change a liquid of mass m kg at its boiling point into vapour is given by the following relationship.*

$$E_h = mL_v$$

In this case L_v is the specific latent heat of vaporisation of the liquid.

15. *Carry out calculations involving specific latent heat of fusion and specific latent heat of vaporisation.*

An example of the kind of calculating that might be expected of you is as follows.

An electric kettle delivers 2000 W of power to boiling water. The specific latent heat of vaporisation of water is $2 \cdot 26 \times 10^6$ J/kg. How much steam is produced in 100 s?

$E_h = power \times time$
$\quad = 2000 \times 100$

$E_h = mL_v$

$m \ = \dfrac{E_h}{L_v}$

$\quad = \dfrac{2000 \times 100}{2 \cdot 26 \times 10^6}$

$\quad = 0 \cdot 09 \; kilogram$

Mass of steam produced is $0 \cdot 09$ kilogram.

UNIT 7 — SPACE PHYSICS

Section	Content
1. Signals from space	Astronomical terms and measurements
	Refracting telescope
	Spectroscopy
	Invisible radiation
	Electromagnetic spectrum
2. Space travel	Rockets
	Interplanetary flight
	Newton's Third Law
	Inertia and mass
	Acceleration due to gravity and gravitational field strength
	Weight
	Free fall and weightlessness
	Satellite motion
	Re-entry and conservation of energy

The paragraphs in italics describe the additional knowledge which is needed for the Credit Level examination.

SECTION 1:   SIGNALS FROM SPACE

Astronomical terms and measurements

1. You should be able to use correctly the terms universe, stars, galaxy, solar system, sun, planet and moon.

   The universe is the name which is given to the whole of space. The universe is made up of billions of large clusters of stars. A large cluster of stars is called a galaxy. A galaxy is made up of billions of stars.

   Stars are enormous masses of very hot gas. Stars emit radiation, some of it in the form of visible light. Our sun is one star in one of the many galaxies that make up the universe.

   Orbiting the sun are large solid objects called planets.

   Orbiting some of the planets are smaller objects called moons.

   The sun and the nine planets which orbit it make up what is called the solar system.

2. The distances between the planets in our solar system are large. However, these distances are small when compared with the distance to the nearest star or the distance across a galaxy. Astronomical distances are hard to imagine. However, their size can be appreciated by representing the distances in terms of the time taken to cover them when travelling at the speed of light.

   The table below gives some typical astronomical distances measured in terms of the time it would take light to travel that distance.

Distance	Time taken for light to travel the distance
Earth to sun Earth to nearest star Diameter of our galaxy (The Milky Way)	8 minutes 4 years 100 000 years

3. *When describing astronomical distances, it is convenient to use a unit of distance called the light-year. A light-year is the distance*

123

which you would cover in 1 year if you travelled at the speed of light.

1 light-year = distance travelled by light in 1 year
= speed of light × number of seconds in 1 year
= 3 × 10⁸ × 365 × 24 × 60 × 60
= 9·5 × 10¹⁵ m

Refracting telescope

4. A refracting telescope is one which uses the refracting property of lenses to form images of objects. The refracting telescope, which is used for astronomy, consists basically of a light tight tube with a long focal length objective lens and a shorter focal length eyepiece lens. The length of the tube can be altered to enable the image to be brought into focus. A diagram of a refracting telescope is shown below.

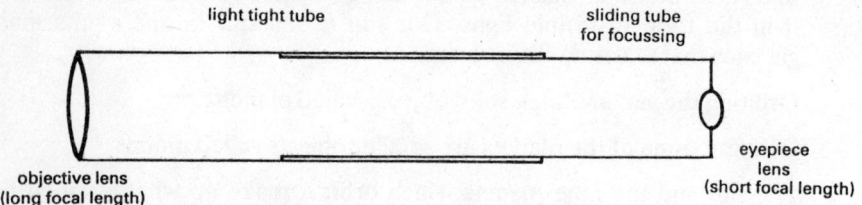

Make sure that you can draw and label this diagram.

5. The objective lens of the telescope forms an image of the object which is being viewed. This image acts as an object for the eyepiece lens. The eyepiece lens then produces a magnified image.

6. *The eyepiece lens of the telescope acts like a magnifying glass. Make sure that you can draw a ray diagram, such as the one below, showing how a magnifying glass forms a magnified image of an object.*

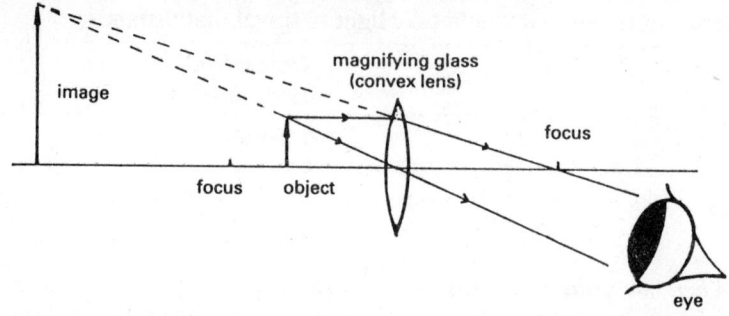

124

Note that in order for the eyepiece to act as a magnifying glass, the object is placed a distance from the lens which is less than the focal length of the lens.

7. The brightness of the image which is formed by a telescope depends on the size of the diameter of the objective lens. The bigger the diameter of the objective lens, the greater the amount of light it can collect from the object being viewed. The greater the amount of light entering the telescope, the brighter the image which is formed.

Spectroscopy

8. When white light, such as that coming from the sun or a lamp, is passed through a prism or a spectroscope, the light is split up into a whole range of colours. The different colours and shades all merge into one another in a continuous way. The range of colours, from red at one end through merging shades of orange, yellow and green to blue at the other end, is called a 'continuous specctrum'.

   The different colours correspond to light of different wavelengths. The red at one end of the spectrum has the longest wavelength, the blue at the other has the shortest wavelength and the green light has a wavelength somewhere in between.

9. The light from some sources, when passed through a prism or spectroscope, produces separated, distinct lines of colour rather than a continuous spectrum. A 'line spectrum', as the separate lines of colour are called, provides information about the atoms in the source of the light. The lines of colour in the spectrum are characteristic of the atoms which are present in the source. The line spectrum is a kind of 'finger-print' of the atoms which are present in the source.

Invisible radiation

10. The visible radiation coming to us from space is just one member of a large family of electromagnetic radiations which reach us. The other members of the family have a range of different wavelengths which cannot be detected by the human eye — they are invisible radiations. All of the radiations travel through space at the same speed as that of visible radiation, i.e. they all travel at the speed of light.

Electromagnetic spectrum

11. The members of the electromagnetic spectrum can be classified as given in the list below. The list is in order of **increasing** wavelength and **decreasing** frequency, i.e. gamma rays have the smallest wavelength and the highest frequency.

    gamma rays; X-rays; ultraviolet radiation; visible radiation; infrared radiation; microwaves; TV waves; radio waves.

12. An example of a detector for each member of the electromagnetic spectrum is given below.

Radiation	*Detector*
Gamma radiation	Geiger Muller tube; photographic film
X-rays	photographic film
ultraviolet radiation	fluorescent materials
visible radiation	human eye; photoelectric cells; photographic film
infrared radiation	photoelectric cells
microwaves	aerial connected to tuned circuit
TV waves	aerial connected to tuned circuit
radio waves	aerial connected to tuned circuit

13. Astronomers are interested in the history and origin of the universe. Information about the universe comes to us from deep space, and reaches us here on the surface of the Earth not only in the form of visible light but also as radio waves. Telescopes have been built which can view the sky and 'see' in the radio frequency part of the electromagnetic spectrum. The giant telescope at Jodrell Bank is a famous example of a radio telescope.

    However, there are also other radiations reaching the Earth from outer space which are of interest to astronomers. These include X-rays, ultraviolet radiation and infrared radiation. All of these radiations can give astronomers clues about what stars and galaxies are made of and how the universe has evolved.

    Different kinds of telescope have been built to detect the different types of radiation. These telescopes carry out their observations from orbiting satellites. This is because X-rays, ultraviolet and infrared radiation tend to be absorbed in the upper part of the Earth's atmosphere and observations from ground level are therefore not possible.

By using different types of telescopes to detect the different wavelengths of radiation from space, a map of the sky can be built up showing the position of sources which emit radiation in different parts of the electromagnetic spectrum.

SECTION 2: SPACE TRAVEL

Rockets

1. A basic rule about the forces which are involved with rockets is as follows.

    "If A pushes on B, then B must push back on A in the opposite direction."

    For example, if a rocket is to be accelerated upwards at lift-off, it needs something to push upwards on it. This something is hot exhaust gas. The rocket motors push hot gas backwards out of the rocket. The hot gas pushes back on the rocket in the opposite direction. The push of the gas on the rocket provides the thrust which enables the rocket to accelerate upwards.

2. You are expected to be able to explain some simple situations involving the rocket rule described above. For example, you should be able to explain the motion which takes place when the air is released from a balloon attached to a straw on a taut thread as shown in the diagram below.

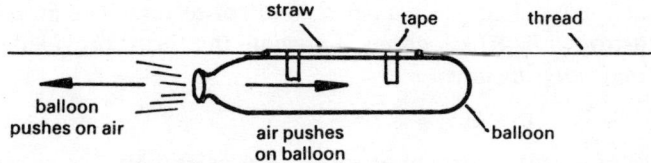

127

Air is pushed out of the balloon to the left. The air pushes back on the balloon to the right. The push from the air provides an unbalanced force which accelerates the balloon along the thread.

The motion of a spring-loaded trolley is another example of a situation which can be explained in terms of the simple rocket rule.

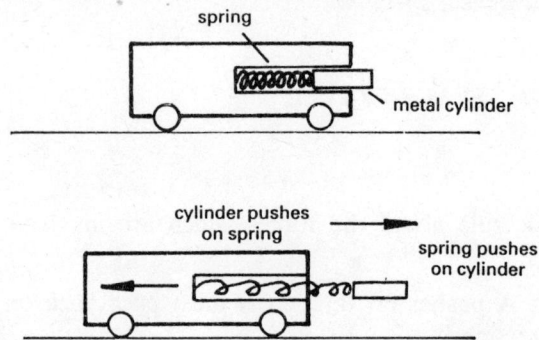

When the spring in the trolley is released, the spring pushes on a metal cylinder. The cylinder pushes back on the spring. The spring and trolley are pushed one way and the cylinder is pushed so that it moves in the opposite direction to the trolley.

3. Carry out calculations involving the thrust, mass and acceleration of rockets. Thrust, mass and acceleration are connected with Newton's Second Law (F = ma).

An example of the kind of calculating that might be expected of you is as follows.

Small rockets on an astronaut's manoeuvring unit are used to accelerate the astronaut in space. The acceleration of the astronaut is 1·5 metres per second per second. The mass of the astronaut is 80 kilograms. Calculate the thrust provided by the manoeuvring unit.

$$F = m \times a$$

thrust of rocket = mass of astronaut × acceleration

thrust = 80 × 1·5
       = 120 newtons

Interplanetary flight

4. Rocket motors are needed to provide an unbalanced force on the rocket so that it can accelerate. However, the rocket motors do not need to be used in order to keep the rocket moving when it is in space. In space, where the rocket's motion is not affected by friction or gravitational forces, the rocket moves in accordance with Newton's First Law. This is the Law which states that if no forces act on an object and that object is moving, the object will continue to move at a constant speed in a straight line.

Newton's Third Law

5. *Newton's Third Law is a more precise statement of the rocket rule given in paragraph 1, Section 2: Space Travel.*

    The Third Law states that if A exerts a force on B, then B will exert an equal and opposite force on A.

6. *At Credit Level, you are expected to be able to identify the 'A force' and the corresponding 'B force' in situations where several forces are acting. The 'A force' and the 'B force' are sometimes referred to as a 'Newton-pair'.*

    Consider, for example, the forces acting on a racing car as it accelerates from rest at the start of a grand prix. This is a situation which involves several forces. Three forces act on the car. These are shown in the diagram below.

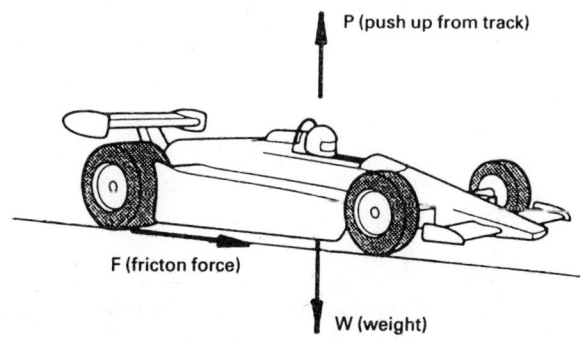

P and W are equal and opposite forces, but they are not a Newton-pair. In fact, none of the combinations of P, W and F are Newton-

pairs because all three act on the same object, the car. Newton-pairs must act on different objects.

P is the upwards push by the track on the car. The other force which makes up the Newton-pair is the downwards push of the car on the track.

The force W is the attractive pull that the Earth has on the car. The force which partners W in a Newton-pair is the upwards pull that the car has for the Earth.

The force F is a friction force which acts on the tyres of the wheels which drive the car. It is the friction force between the tyres and track which pushes the car forwards. For example, if the car started on a patch of oil, there would be no friction between tyre and track. The tyres would slip and spin and there would be no forward motion of the car.

The Newton-pair partner for force F is the backwards push of the tyres on the track.

Inertia and mass

7. *Inertia means a disinclination to move or act — an unwillingness to change.*

   Matter can be thought of as having inertia in the sense that it demonstrates an unwillingess to change its state of motion. Objects at rest tend to stay at rest or, if they are moving, they tend to continue moving in a straight line at a constant speed. The objects exhibit an opposition to any change in their motion — i.e. they resist being accelerated.

   The more mass an object has, the greater the inertia of the object. An object's mass is a measure of the object's inertia. An object of mass 1000 kg, for example, has more inertia than an object of mass 1 kg. Changing the motion of a mass of 1000 kg is much more difficult than doing the same for a mass of 1 kg.

Acceleration due to gravity and gravitational field strength

8. All objects falling freely, i.e. where there is little or no air resistance, near the Earth's surface have the same acceleration.

It is the weight of the object, i.e. the Earth's gravitational pull on the object, which produces the acceleration. The acceleration is called the 'acceleration due to gravity' or the 'gravitational acceleration'.

9. *Using Newton's Second Law (F = ma), we can express the weight of an object in terms of its mass and the acceleration due to gravity as follows.*

Weight (N) = mass (kg) × acceleration due to gravity (m/s²)

The weight of the same object can also be expressed in terms of the mass of the object and the gravitational field strength as follows.

Weight (N) = mass (kg) × gravitational field strength (N/kg)

Therefore, acceleration due to gravity in the first expression must be equivalent to gravitational field strength in the second expression. Acceleration due to gravity and gravitational field strength have the same numerical value. They are just two different ways of expressing the same thing. Sometimes it will be convenient to use gravitational field strength and the value 10 N/kg in doing a calculation. On other occasions it will be perhaps more appropriate to use acceleration due to gravity and the value 10 m/s².

Weight

10. The weight of an object, i.e. the force acting on the object due to the gravitational pull of the Earth, gets less the further the object is away from the Earth's surface.

11. The weight of an object on the moon or on another planet in the solar system, i.e. the force acting on the object due to the gravitational pull from the moon or the planet, is different from its weight on earth.

12. *Carry out calculations involving the relationship w = mg (where g is given as the acceleration due to gravity or the gravitational field strength) in situations where 'g' is not 10 N/kg or 10 m/s².*

An example of the kind of calculating that might be expected of you is as follows.

131

(a) Calculate the weight of an astronaut of mass 80 kg at a height above the Earth's surface where the Earth's gravitational field strength is 3 N/kg.

$w = mg$

$w = 80 \times 3$

$\quad = 240 \ N$

weight of astronaut = 240 N

(b) What is the acceleration due to gravity at this height?

The values for gravitational field strength and acceleration due to gravity are the same. Therefore acceleration due to gravity is 3 m/s².

Free fall and weightlessness

13. Objects which fall freely under the influence of a gravitational pull only appear to be 'weightless'. It is, however, the free fall condition which gives rise to the appearance. The objects are not truly weightless — they are still acted upon by a gravitational pull — objects in free-fall do have weight.

For example, objects in a space shuttle are seen to float. The objects, however, are simply in free fall. The objects and every other object around them are falling with the same acceleration. The objects therefore float relative to each other. They appear weightless.

14. Projectile motion can be thought of as an example of a free fall motion. If air resistance is ignored, then the only force acting on a projectile after it is launched is the force of gravity. As the projectile moves outwards it is being pulled downwards by the force of gravity. A combination of these two motions gives rise to a curved flight path.

15. *At Credit Level, you are expected to be able to explain projectile motion in terms of two motions — a horizontal, constant speed motion and a vertical, constant acceleration motion.*

Imagine a projectile, such as a marble, is launched horizontally from a table top. The curved path followed by the marble can be explained as follows.

The path can be thought of as comprising two motions which are not dependent on each other. One is a horizontal motion and the other is a vertical motion.

If the air resistance forces acting on the marble are negligible, then there are no forces acting on the marble in a horizontal direction. Therefore, the motion in that direction obeys Newton's First Law, i.e. the marble moves with a constant horizontal speed.

The vertical motion is a constant acceleration. The acceleration is provided by the only vertically acting force — the projectile's weight. The combination of the constant horizontal speed and the constant downwards vertical acceleration gives rise to a special type of curved path called a parabola.

16. You should be able to make use of the fact that projectile motion can be considered as two independent motions and carry out calculations on this type of motion.

An example of the kind of calculating that might be expected of you is as follows.

A marble is launched from a height h with a horizontal speed of 3 m/s as shown below. The marble travels a horizontal distance of 0·9 m before hitting the ground as shown in the diagram below.

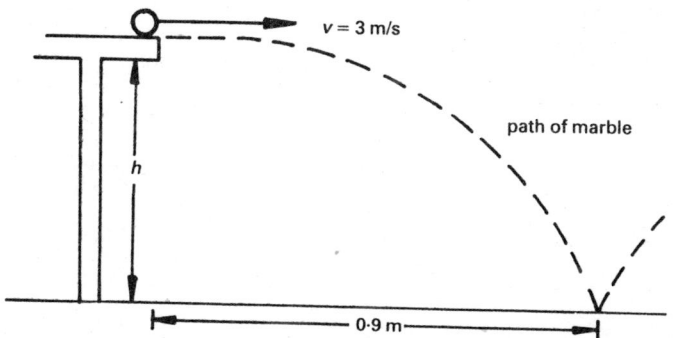

The acceleration due to gravity can be taken to be 10 m/s² and the effects of air resistance on the motion may be neglected.

Calculate
(i) the time of flight of the marble;
(ii) the vertical speed of the marble on reaching the ground;
(iii) the height h.

133

(i) horizontal distance = horizontal speed × flight time
                         = 3 × flight time

$$flight\ time = \frac{0 \cdot 9}{3}$$

                         = 0·3 s

(ii) The vertical motion is a constant acceleration of 10 m/s². The object takes 0·3 s to reach the ground.

$$a = \frac{v - u}{t}$$

$$10 = \frac{v - 0}{0 \cdot 3}$$

$$v = 10 \times 0 \cdot 3$$

$$= 3\ m/s$$

vertical speed of marble = 3 m/s

(iii) The vertical motion is a constant acceleration and can be described by the following speed-time graph.

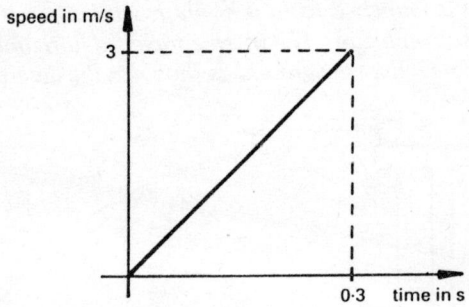

distance travelled vertically = area under speed-time graph

$$= \frac{1}{2} \times 0 \cdot 3 \times 3$$

$$= 0 \cdot 45\ m$$

height (h) = 0·45 m

Satellite motion

17. Satellite motion can be thought of as a kind of projectile motion.

    For example, suppose a cannonball is fired horizontally from a high *mountain. The cannonball falls towards the Earth as it travels outwards from the mountain. The path followed by the cannonball is an example of projective motion. The bigger the launch speed of the cannonball, the further it travels outwards from the mountain as shown in the diagram below.*

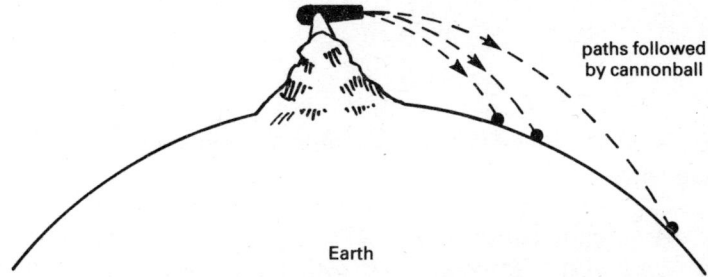

paths followed by cannonball

Earth

If the launch speed is made large enough, then the cannonball can be projected so that it travels beyond the horizon and misses the 'edge' of the Earth.

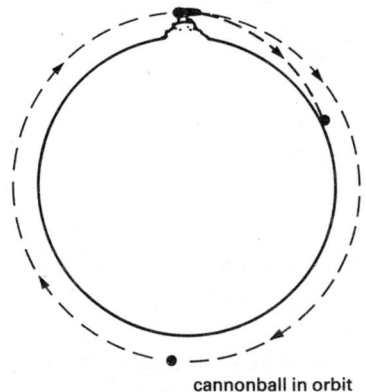

cannonball in orbit

The cannonball still continues to fall towards the Earth with a constant acceleration but its speed is such that it keeps missing the Earth as it falls.

The high speed cannonball behaves like a low altitude satellite.

18. When a spacecraft re-enters the earth's atmosphere a friction force acts on the spacecraft. Work is done against this friction force. The kinetic energy of the spacecraft decreases. Energy is transferred as heat.

Re-entry and conservation of energy

19. *Carry out calculations involving conservation of energy and the following relationships.*

$$E_h = cm\Delta T$$
$$W = Fd$$
$$E_k = \frac{1}{2}mv^2$$

An example of the kind of calculating that might be expected of you is as follows.

A lump of debris of mass 250 kg from space enters the Earth's atmosphere. Over the first 600 m of its journey through the atmosphere it experiences a friction force of 3×10^5 N. The specific heat capacity of the debris material is 900 J/kg °C.

Calculate, for this first 600 m of its entry into the Earth's atmosphere,

(i) the loss in kinetic energy of the debris;

(ii) the increase in the temperature of the debris material.

(i) work done against friction force = Fd

$$Fd = 3 \times 10^5 \times 600$$
$$= 1 \cdot 8 \times 10^8 \, J$$

loss in kinetic energy = work done against friction
loss in kinetic energy = $1 \cdot 8 \times 10^8 \, J$

(ii) energy transferred = work done against friction
$$= heat \, produced$$
$$= cm\Delta T$$

$$cm\Delta T = 1 \cdot 8 \times 10^8$$
$$\Delta T = \frac{1 \cdot 8 \times 10^8}{250 \times 900}$$
$$= 800 \, °C$$

increase in temperature of debris material = 800 °C

RELATIONSHIPS TO REMEMBER

The relationships which are identified by an asterisk ($\star$) are needed for the General Level examination.

All of the relationships are needed for the Credit Level examination.

Telecommunication

$\star$ speed = $\dfrac{\text{distance}}{\text{time}}$ .... $v = \dfrac{d}{t}$

$\star$ wave speed = frequency $\times$ wavelength .... $v = f\lambda$

Using Electricity and Electronics

$\star$ resistance = $\dfrac{\text{voltage}}{\text{current}}$ .... $R = \dfrac{V}{I}$

$\star$ power = $\dfrac{\text{energy transferred}}{\text{time}}$ .... $P = \dfrac{E}{t}$

$\star$ power = voltage $\times$ current .... $P = VI$

$\star$ In a series circuit, current is everywhere the same.

$\star$ In a series circuit, voltage of supply equals sum of voltages across each component. .... $V = V_1 + V_2$

$\star$ In a parallel circuit, voltage across components in parallel is the same.

$\star$ In a parallel circuit, current from supply = sum of currents in branches. .... $I = I_1 + I_2$

$\star$ voltage gain of an amplifier = $\dfrac{\text{voltage output}}{\text{voltage input}}$

charge = current $\times$ time .... $Q = It$

resistance of resistors in series .... $R_s = R_1 + R_2$

resistance of resistors in parallel .... $\dfrac{1}{R_p} = \dfrac{1}{R_1} + \dfrac{1}{R_2}$

power = current^2 $\times$ resistance .... $P = I^2R$

power = $\dfrac{\text{voltage}^2}{\text{resistance}}$ .... $P = \dfrac{V^2}{R}$

power gain of an amplifier = $\dfrac{\text{power output}}{\text{power input}}$

Health Physics

$$\text{power of a lens} = \frac{1}{\text{focal length}}$$

half-life = time taken for activity to reduce by half

Transport and Space Physics

★ average speed $= \dfrac{\text{distance travelled}}{\text{time taken}}$ .... $v = \dfrac{d}{t}$

★ acceleration $= \dfrac{\text{change in speed}}{\text{time taken for change}}$ .... $a = \dfrac{v - u}{t}$

★ weight in newtons = mass in kilograms × 10 ....

★ force = mass × acceleration .... $F = ma$

★ work done = force × distance .... $W = Fd$

★ power $= \dfrac{\text{work done}}{\text{time}}$ .... $P = \dfrac{W}{t}$

★ power $= \dfrac{\text{energy transferred}}{\text{time}}$ .... $P = \dfrac{E}{t}$

★ gravitational potential energy
   = mass × gravitational field strength × height ... $E_p = mgh$

★ heat supplied = specific heat capacity
                    × mass × temperature rise .... $E_h = cm\Delta T$

distance travelled = area under a speed-time graph

kinetic energy $= \dfrac{1}{2} \times$ mass × speed^2 .... $E_k = \dfrac{1}{2}mv^2$

gravitational field strength $= \dfrac{\text{weight}}{\text{mass}}$ .... $g = \dfrac{w}{m}$

value of gravitational field strength
      =value of acceleration due to gravity

Energy Matters

★ gravitational potential energy
= mass × gravitational field strength × height ... $E_p = mgh$

★ $\dfrac{\text{secondary voltage}}{\text{primary voltage}} = \dfrac{\text{number of turns on secondary}}{\text{number of turns on primary}}$ $\dfrac{V_s}{V_p} = \dfrac{N_s}{N_p}$

★ power = $\dfrac{\text{energy transferred}}{\text{time}}$ .... $P = \dfrac{E}{t}$

★ heat supplied = specific heat capacity
× mass × temperature rise .... $E_h = cm\Delta T$

efficiency of a power station
$= \dfrac{\text{energy transferred at output}}{\text{energy delivered at input}}$

efficiency of a transformer
$= \dfrac{\text{power obtained from secondary}}{\text{power delivered to primary}} = \dfrac{V_s \times I_s}{V_p \times I_p}$

power = $\dfrac{\text{voltage}^2}{\text{resistance}}$ .... $P = \dfrac{V^2}{R}$

specific latent heat of fusion
$= \dfrac{\text{heat supplied to change state (solid to liquid)}}{\text{mass changing state}}$ .. $L_f = \dfrac{E_h}{m}$

specific latent heat of vaporisation
$= \dfrac{\text{heat supplied to change state (liquid to vapour)}}{\text{mass changing state}}$ $L_v = \dfrac{E_h}{m}$

KNOWLEDGE AND UNDERSTANDING
QUESTIONS AND ANSWERS

The following questions, **except** those in italics, test your knowledge and understanding of content which is needed for the General Level examination.

All of the questions test the knowledge and understanding which is required for the Credit Level examination.

QUESTIONS

Unit 1

1. The diagram below is intended to show how the parts of a TV receiver are put together. Some of the labels on the diagram have got mixed up.

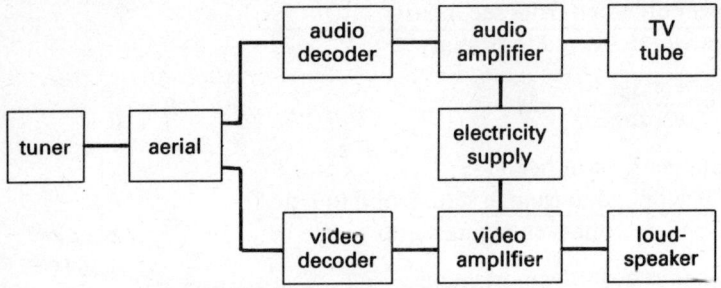

Redraw the diagram with the labels in the correct boxes.

2. A musical note of frequency Y is paired with a note of frequency Z as shown in the table below.

	Frequency Y in hertz	Frequency Z in hertz
A	250	350
B	250	251
C	250	249
D	250	150
E	250	125

In which pair are the notes one octave apart?

3. *A radio station broadcasts on a frequency of 600 kHz. What is the wavelength of the broadcast?*

4. A beam of electrons can be made to scan the screen of a TV tube. The scanning beam traces lines on the screen as shown in the diagram.

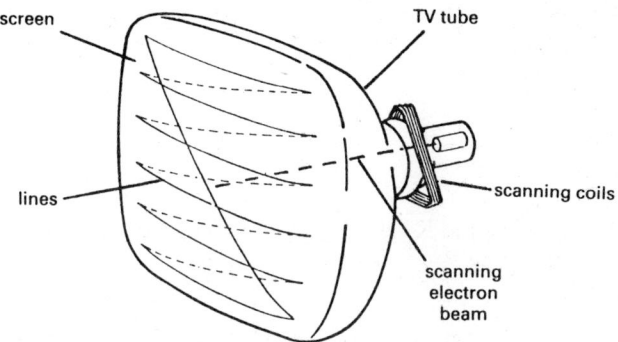

Describe how the scanning beam and the lines can form a picture on the screen.

5. *(a)* What is an optical fibre?

   (b) Describe how optical fibres can be used for telecommunication.

6. *The diagram below shows a ray of light travelling between A and B in part of an optical fibre. The path which is followed by the ray between B and C is not shown.*

Complete the diagram to show the path followed by the ray in travelling from B to C.

Unit 2

7. The power of an electric kettle is likely to be approximately

A 50 watts
B 100 watts
C 240 watts
D 2000 watts
E 20 000 watts.

8 What is meant by
   (i) alternating current;
   (ii) direct current?

9. Two resistors R_1 and R_2 are connected to an electrical supply as shown in the diagram below.

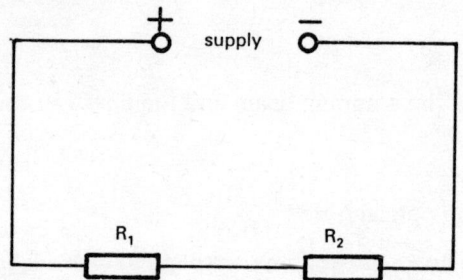

The current in R_2 and the voltage of the supply have to be measured.

Redraw and complete the circuit diagram showing where an ammeter and voltmeter are connected to enable the measurements to be made.

10. The energy transferred by an electric current is measured by a domestic electricity meter in

A volts
B amperes
C ohms
D kilowatt-hours
E watts.

11. *(a) Describe, using a circuit diagram, a household ring circuit.*

    (b) State two differences between the household ring circuit and the circuit which is used for household lighting.

142

12. *(a)* The diagram shows a simple electric motor.

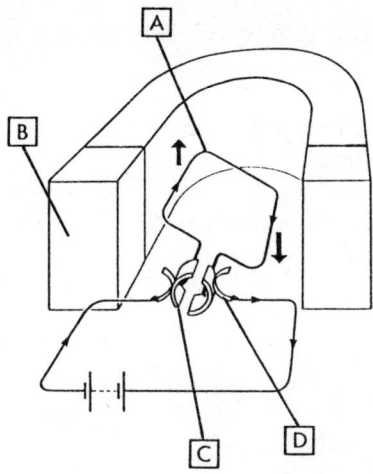

Name the parts of the motor which are labelled A, B, C and D in the diagram.

(b) *The coil of the motor rotates in an anti-clockwise direction. State two ways of changing the direction of rotation.*

13. An electric blanket is connected to a 240 volt supply. The power of the blanket is 120 watts. What is the current in the blanket?

14. Fluorescent tube lamps are advertised as being more efficient than filament lamps. Describe what is meant by 'more efficient'.

15. *The circuit diagrams for circuit X and circuit Y are shown below. Do a calculation to show which circuit has the greater resistance.*

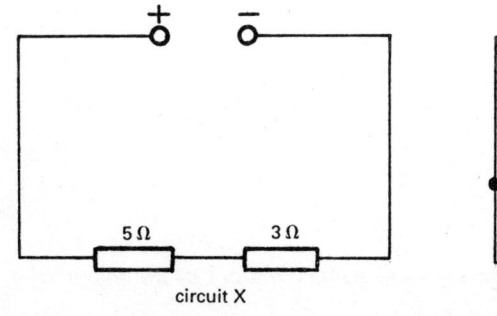

circuit X

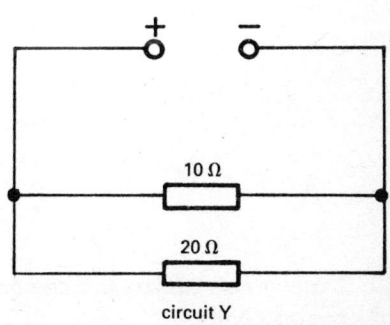

circuit Y

143

16. Describe the main differences between a clinical thermometer and a common mercury thermometer.

17. State a typical value for the sound level at the ear of the listener during normal conversation.

18. A convex lens is used as shown in the diagram below to focus rays of light from an object on to a screen.

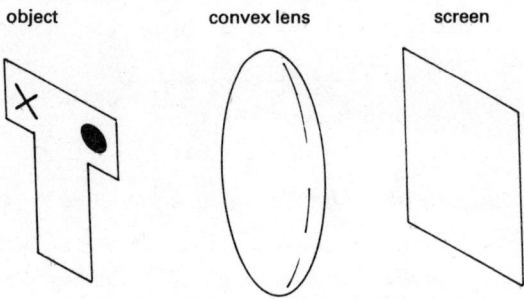

Which of the following diagrams represents the image which is formed on the screen?

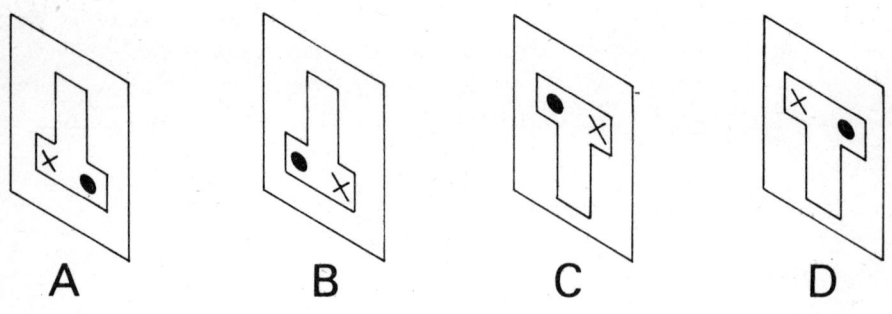

19. *Explain how ultrasound can be used to produce images of the inside of a person's body*

144

20. *The graph below shows how the activity of a radioactive source varies with time.*

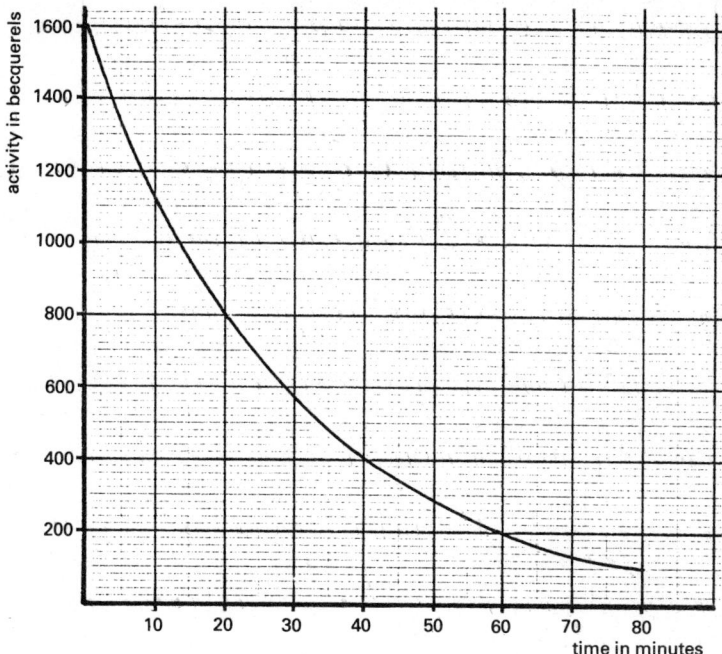

What is the half-life of the source?

21. Name an output device which produces
    (i) light;
    (ii) sound;
    (iii) movement.

22. A light emitting diode is connected in series with a resistor R to a 5 volt d.c. supply as shown in the diagram below.

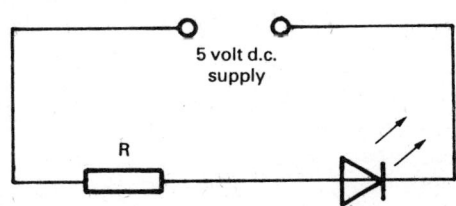

(a) Which terminal (left or right) is the + side of the supply?

(b) What is the purpose of the resistor R?

(c) The current in the LED is 12 mA and the voltage across it is 2 V. What is the resistance of R?

23. Which one of the circuit diagrams shown below is for a time delay? State a use for the circuit represented by the other diagram.

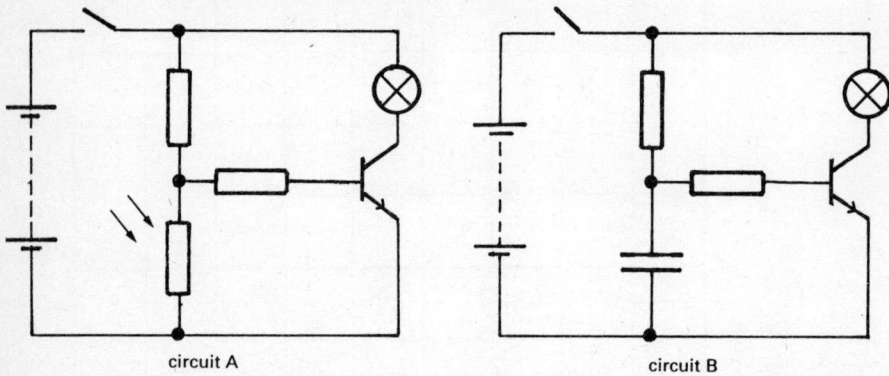

circuit A   circuit B

24. *The resistance of the thermistor in the diagram below becomes lower as its temperature increases. The diagram represents the circuit for a simple fire alarm.*

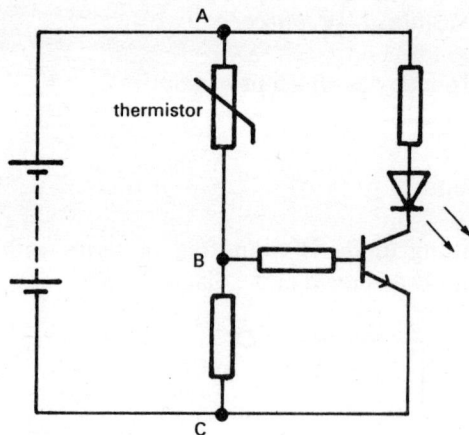

Explain how the circuit works.

25. Sketch the symbol for
   (i) a two-input AND gate;
   (ii) a NOT gate.

26. *Name the two-input gate which has the following truth table.*

Input		Output
A	B	C
0	0	0
0	1	1
1	0	1
1	1	1

27. The block diagram shown below represents a counting circuit.

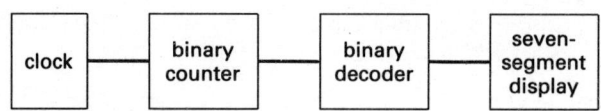

What is the purpose of
   (i) the binary decoder;
   (ii) the seven-segment display?

28. *A loudspeaker of resistance R ohms is connected to the output of an amplifier. The amplifier supplies a voltage V to the loudspeaker.*

The power delivered to the loudspeaker is

A $\dfrac{V}{R}$

B VR

C $\dfrac{V^2}{R}$

D V^2R

E $\dfrac{R}{V^2}.$

29. What is meant by
    (i) average speed;
    (ii) instantaneous speed?

30. Describe a way of measuring the instantaneous speed of an object.

31. A car is travelling at a constant speed. It then accelerates uniformly before again travelling at a constant speed. The car then decelerates uniformly and comes to a stop.

    Sketch a speed-time graph of the motion described above.

32. *(a)* State Newton's First Law.

    (b) Give an example of a situation where Newton's First Law applies. Name the forces which are involved.

33. Use Newton's Laws to explain the need for the wearing of car seat belts.

34. *A parachutist of mass 75 kg jumps from an aircraft. Just before the parachute is opened, an air resistance force of 450 newtons acts on the parachutist.*

    (a) What is the weight of the parachutist?

    (b) Calculate the acceleration of the parachutist just before the parachute is opened.

35. *A stone is dropped down a deep well. The stone takes 2 seconds to reach the water at the bottom of the well. The stone has an acceleration of 10 m/s^2 throughout its fall.*

    (a) What is the speed of the stone just before it reaches the water in the well?

    (b) Sketch a speed-time graph of the motion of the stone.

    (c) Calculate the distance from the top of the well to the surface of the water.

36. A toy car is given a push so that it moves along the frictionless track shown in the diagram below.

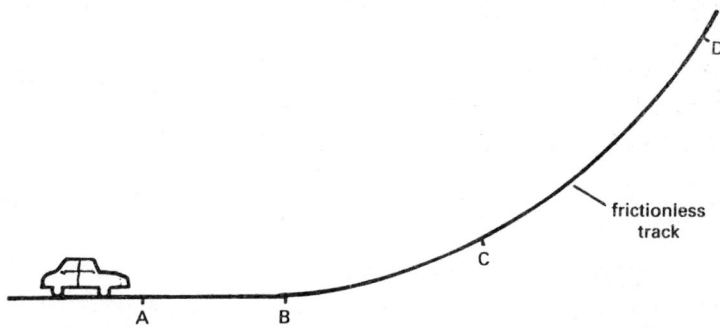

The car moves with a constant speed between A and B at the bottom of the track. It then travels up the track past C and reaches D, from where it rolls back down the track.

Where in the travel of the car does the car have

(a) maximum kinetic energy;

(b) maximum gravitational potential energy;

(c) both kinetic and potential energy;

(d) no acceleration?

37. A cyclist of mass of 70 kilograms has an acceleration of 1·5 metres per second per second. Calculate the size of the unbalanced force acting on the cyclist.

38. *Which of the trolleys shown in the diagram below has the greatest acceleration?*

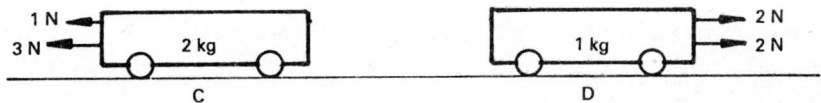

39. *A car of mass 1200 kg accelerates from rest to reach a speed of 25 m/s in 8 s.*

   (a) *Calculate the kinetic energy of the car at 25 m/s.*

   (b) *How much work is done on the car during the 8 s?*

   (c) *Calculate the power developed by the car's engine.*

Unit 6

40. *Energy is 'conserved'. This being the case, there can be no truth in the statement that the world is running out of energy. What is it that is happening to energy?*

41. Describe how a pumped hydro-electric scheme works.

42. *Explain, using a diagram, what is meant by a chain reaction.*

43. Waste material is produced from the fuel used in a nuclear power station. This waste cannot be dumped in the same way as the waste material produced by a power station which uses fossil fuel. What type of waste is produced from a nuclear power station?

44. *State three factors which affect the size of the voltage induced in a coil which is rotating in a magnetic field.*

45. A pupil decides to assemble a simple transformer. What components are needed to make up a transformer?

46. *Explain why transformers are never 100% efficient.*

47. *A transformer delivers a current of 3 A to a lamp. The voltage across the lamp is 12 V. The primary coil of the transformer is connected to a mains supply of 240 V. The current in the primary coil is 144 mA.*

   Calculate the efficiency of the transformer.

48. What is meant by the specific heat capacity of a substance?

49. The specific heat capacity of a metal block is 880 joules per kilogram per degree celsius. The block has a mass of 0·2 kilograms. How much heat must be supplied to the block to raise its temperature from 10 degrees celsius to 50 degrees celsius?

50. *An electric kettle has a power of 2400 W. The kettle holds 1·5 kg of water at 20 °C. Calculate how long it will take the kettle to bring the water to its boiling point. The specific heat capacity of the water is 4200 J/kg °C.*

51. *A heater supplies 250 joules of energy per second.*

   (i) *How long will it take the heater to change 0·1 kg of water at its boiling point into steam?*

   (ii) *How much ice at 0 °C would be melted by the heater in the same time?*

   The specific latent heat of vaporisation of water is 22·6 × 10⁵ J/kg and the specific latent heat of fusion of ice is 3·3 × 10⁵ J/kg.

52. A kettle brings water to its boiling point. The kettle remains switched on. Why does the temperature of the water in the kettle not continue to rise?

53. Complete the following paragraph.

   Latent heat of _____ of ice is the heat which is needed to change ice into _____. Solid changing to _____ is called a change of _____. Such a change does not involve a change of _____.

Unit 7

54. *What is a light-year?*

55. The diagram below shows an astronomical telescope.

151

What is the purpose of

(i) the objective lens,

(ii) the eyepiece lens?

56. Apart from visible radiation, name another radiation from deep space which reaches us on the surface of Earth. Name a detector for this radiation.

57. What basic rule about forces can be used to explain the motion of a rocket at lift-off?

58. A quiz contestant sits motionless in a chair. The forces which act on the contestant are shown in the diagram below.

Force P is the upwards push on the contestant from the chair.

(a) What is force W?

(b) How does the size of force P compare with the size of force W?

(c) *What force is the Newton-pair partner for force P?*

59. *A ball rolls off the end of a bench with a horizontal speed of 0·5 m/s. The ball hits the floor 0·4 s later. The acceleration due to gravity is 10 m/s².*

    (i) Calculate the horizontal distance travelled by the ball between leaving the bench top and hitting the floor.

    (ii) Calculate the vertical speed of the ball just before it hits the floor.

    (iii) Sketch a speed-time graph of the vertical motion of the ball.

    (iv) Calculate the height of the bench.

60. When a space vehicle re-enters the Earth's atmosphere, a friction force acts on the vehicle. State two effects of the friction force on the vehicle.

ANSWERS

The answers to the questions are given mostly in the form of a reference number. The reference number tells you where to look in the book to find the correct answer to the question.

For example, the reference number which is given for question 1 is 1.3.12. This number refers you to Unit 1 (Telecommunication), section 3 (Radio and television), paragraph 12 (Television receiver).

Use the reference number to see how well the answer which you gave to the question matches up to what might be expected of you in the examination.

1. 1.3.12
2. Pair E (1.1.10)
3. 500 m (1.3.9)
4. 1.3.15
5. (a) 1.4.1
   (b) 1.4.1
6. (1.4.5)

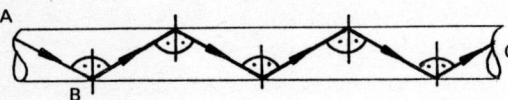

7. Answer D (2.1.2)
8. (i) 2.2.1
   (ii) 2.2.1
9. (2.3.2)

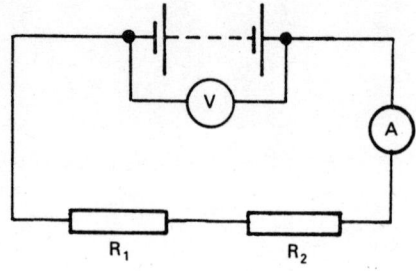

10. Answer D (2.5.6)
11. *(a)* 2.5.2
    (b) 2.5.4
12. *(a)* 2.6.4
    (b) 2.6.2
13. 0·5 ampere (2.3.10)
14. 2.3.13
15. Circuit X (2.4.7)
16. 3.1.2
17. 3.2.6
18. Answer B (3.3.4)
19 3.2.4
20. 20 minutes (3.5.8)
21. 4.2.1
22. *(a)* Left (4.2.5)
    (b) 4.2.6
    (c) 250 Ω (4.2.6)
23. Circuit B; parking light (4.4.2)
24. The thermistor senses the temperature of the air. A fire would cause the air temperature to increase. The resistance of the thermistor would decrease. The voltage at B would increase. The transistor would be switched on. The circuit for the LED is now complete. The LED lights and gives warning of a fire. (4.4.3)
25. (i) 4.4.5
    (ii) 4.4.5
26. OR gate (4.4.6)
27. (i) 4.4.10
    (ii) 4.4.10
28. 4.5.6
29. (i) 5.1.1
    (ii) 5.1.3
30. 5.1.3

31. (5.1.8)

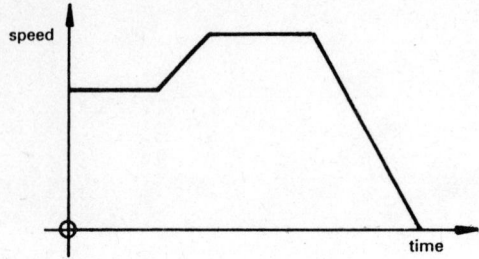

32. *(a)* 5.2.9 *(b)* 5.2.10
33. 5.2.15
34. *(a)* 750 N (5.2.3) *(b)* 4 m/s^2 (5.2.14)
35. *(a)* 20 m/s (5.1.12)
    (b) (5.1.8)

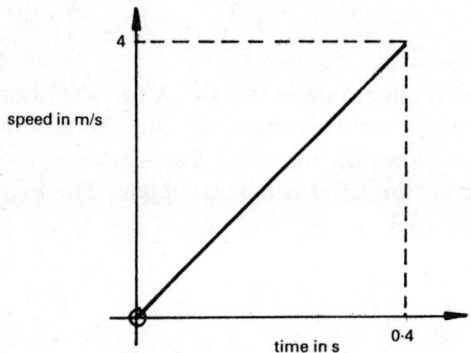

(c) 20 m (5.1.11)
36. *(a)* Between A and B (5.3.1) *(b)* D (5.3.1)
    (c) C (5.3.1) *(d)* Between A and B (5.1.6)
37. 105 newtons (5.2.13)
38. Trolley D (5.2.14)
39. *(a)* 375 000 J (5.3.4) *(b)* 375 000 J (5.3.7) *(c)* 46 875 W (5.3.9)

40. 6.2.4

41. 6.2.7

42. 6.2.8

43. 6.2.9

44. 6.3.4

45. 6.3.5

46. 6.3.8

47. 96% (6.3.9)

48. 6.4.3

49. 7040 joules (6.4.5)

50. 210 seconds (6.4.6)

51.   (i) 904 s (6.4.15)
    (ii) E_h = power × time
$$= 250 \times 1004$$
$$E_h = mL_f$$
$$m = \frac{E_h}{L_f}$$
$$= \frac{250 \times 904}{3 \cdot 3 \times 10^5}$$
$$= 0 \cdot 68 \text{ kg (6.4.15)}$$

52. 6.4.8

53. fusion; water; liquid; state; temperature
(6.4.7; 6.4.8)

54. 7.1.3

55.   (i) 7.1.5
    (ii) 7.1.5

56. 7.1.13; 7.1.12

57. 7.2.1

58. *(a)* Weight (5.2.3)
    (b) P = W (5.2.8)
    (c) The push of the contestant on the chair
(7.2.6)

59. (i) 0·2 m (7.2.16)
     (ii) 4 m/s (5.1.12)
     (iii) (5.1.8)

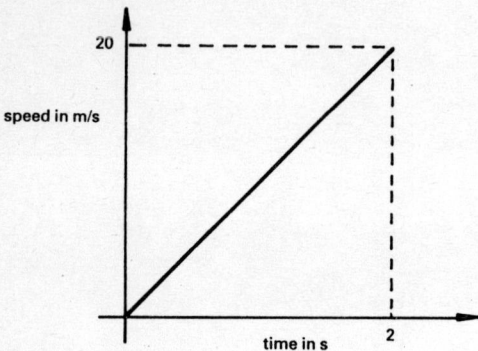

     (iv) 0·8 m (5.1.11)
60. 7.2.18